Orang Utan

Monica Borner
with Bernard Stonehouse

Orang Utan
Orphans of the Forest

Book Club Associates
London

For
Dr R. FAUST
whose confidence in us and understanding
of our problems helped us to overcome
many difficulties.

The Television Programme

'World of Survival's' television Special, 'Orang Utan, Orphans of the Forest' has been seen by approximately 140 million television viewers all over the world. Narrated by Peter Ustinov, the film shot by Survival wildlife camera team Dieter Plage and Mike Price took over six months to make. Conditions in the thick rain forest of the Gunung Leuser Reserve in Sumatra were so humid that by the end of that time tentage and clothes had rotted and fungus had even found its way between the elements of the camera lenses.

Contents

Illustrations

Photographs numbered 1–6, 8, 10–14, 16–19, 21–23, 29–32, 34 are by Monica Borner; 7, 15, 20, 35 are by Regina Frey; 9, 28, 33 are by Dieter Plage; 24–27 are by Colin Willock.

Maps

'Help for Threatened Wildlife'

It all started with the Serengeti. The need to do more about the world-wide protection of wildlife became clear back in the 1940s, but it was the work of Bernhard Grzimek and his son Michael whose research on the Serengeti in the late 1950s gave shape to these intentions and provided the impulse for the Frankfurt Zoological Society to widen its scope. Since then the Zoologische Gesellschaft von 1858, Frankfurt am Main has administered a separate fund under the slogan 'Help for Threatened Wildlife' and has become a well known and widely active nature conservancy organization. Concentrating first on East and Central Africa, the Society now operates world-wide.

More and more throughout the world, species, animal ecology and whole landscapes are being threatened. In the last resort these threats turn back on the species that poses them – man. Thus everyone everywhere needs to do something about the conservation of nature and its creatures. We must all come to see nature conservancy and environmental protection as a cultural and moral responsibility.

The Frankfurt Zoological Society's aim is to make the best use of its resources in containing damage which has occurred and where possible remedying it. At a total expenditure of over $5m the Society has implemented or supported conservation projects in many countries of South East Asia, Africa, South America and Europe. This may sound good but it is not enough. As Hermann Löns said in 1811: 'The destruction of nature is a wholesale operation, its protection a retail one.'

The orang utan project which is the subject of this book was and is still being funded by the Society.

Monica Borner

Zoologische Gesellschaft von 1858
Alfred-Brehm-Platz 16
6000 Frankfurt am Main 1

'Help for Threatened Wildlife'
Postal Giro No. 47–601,
Frankfurt am Main

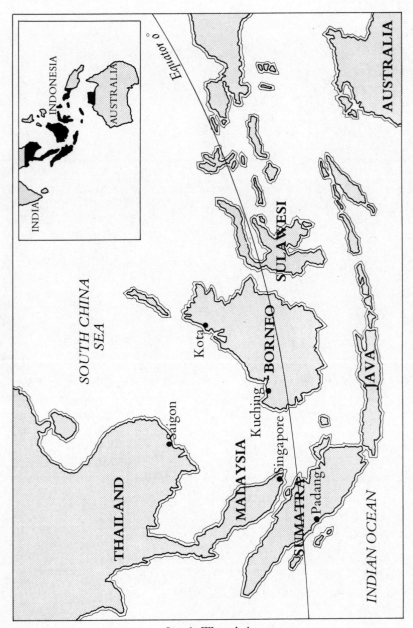

South-West Asia

Orang Utan

I
How it Began

The little orang utan hung high above my head in a tree. He was holding on with his left hand, twisting slowly to left and right. His short legs were drawn up beneath him with feet clasping each other. In his right hand he held a twig, torn from a nearby branch, which he playfully whisked and popped into his mouth from time to time. Now and then he threw a glance toward his mother, who squatted above and to the side of him, half-hidden in the fork of a large branch. Her browny-red fur, darker than that of her baby, merged with the rich brown shadows of the forest.

Motionless in the undergrowth I watched them through the lazy afternoon. Outside the forest the sun beat fiercely; inside it was cool and dim, and soundless but for the buzz of insects and the occasional chirp of cicadas. The two orangs knew I was there, but accepted me philosophically as part of the forest. As a stranger and possible predator I had to be watched, but only in a casual way – while I stayed still and quiet, they were untroubled.

The little one dropped his twig and reached up with his right hand, grasping the branch above his head. Shifting his weight – some 10 to 15 pounds – he swung slowly up and clambered toward his mother. His movements were cautious and hesitant; he still had a lot to learn about climbing and swinging through the tangle of branches and lianas. He climbed to the branch a

I

little above his mother, using his feet, with their long toes and short opposed thumbs, as an extra pair of hands. Then he slid slowly head-first over her shoulder. His lips found one of her nipples among the fur, and in a moment he was sucking greedily. The mother slumped comfortably in her tree fork, munching yellow-green, plum sized fruits from a bunch in her hand. Sucking each fruit with relish, she let the stones fall from her mouth; they plopped down onto the damp, shiny leaves beside me.

It was a happy sight and one I enjoyed watching – two orang utans, free, natural and contented, quietly being themselves in their own native forest. I'd already stayed with them for most of the day, and would follow them through the forest till nightfall. But watching orangs was not just a pastime. In the last few weeks it had become an important part of my daily routine and my life. Watching this mother and baby in the forest close to the Ketambe research station was training – part of my preparation for a task in conservation which had brought me across the world from Switzerland to the green forests of northern Sumatra. My work – specifically the rehabilitation and return to freedom of orangs recovered from captivity – was part of an international campaign to save an animal species from a threat of destruction. Here in the forest I was learning how mother and infant relate to each other, to help me in dealing with the young orangs – many crippled mentally or physically by their handling in captivity – which would soon be entrusted to me.

A group of hornbills moved noisily through the canopy. Suddenly the female orang stood up, dropping the last of her fruit at my feet. In a moment the little one was at her side, clutching her hard with hands and feet locked in her hair. With hands and feet free she moved slowly but easily from branch to branch above my head, swinging, pausing, balancing, clambering, dropping with the skill of an acrobat, seemingly unencumbered by the little one at her side. This was not the spectacular, high-speed acrobatics of the gibbons and leaf-monkeys that had passed our way at noon. It was a leisurely saunter, perhaps using a well-known track through the treetops, which carried her at a steady pace of 1 to 2 miles per hour. I followed on the ground a little way back, tripping over rotten tree trunks, sinking over my ankles in black, cold puddles, and making long detours around thorn thickets. While the orangs moved easily like birds along an almost straight path, I scrambled the hard way up ridges and down gullies; they swung with ease over the top of a ravine, while I took the rough tracks below. Clearly, four hands were better than two feet for negotiating rain forest.

The young orang didn't want to be carried all the time. Two years old and starting to feel his independence, he let go from time to time and followed his mother, using exactly the same branches and handholds. Now and then, if he fell behind, she paused to wait for him and let him catch up. At last they reached their destination – a tall tree with a large orang nest 100 feet up in its branches. The mother swung up to it with the youngster following closely. She broke off a handful of soft young twigs, taking them into the nest with her. Her head and shoulders appeared over the edge, vanishing again as she made herself comfortable. The little one climbed after her hurriedly to a point just a few feet above the nest and dropped in on top of her with a thump. There was a rustling and snapping of twigs as they settled, then all was quiet. I watched for a moment as the shadows deepened, then hurried back to the station before dark.

For me the story began late in 1971. As a finals-year student of Zoology at the University of Zurich I was looking for something interesting and practical to do. On the point of completing my last set of examinations, I wanted to escape from the library and desk, and at last do some fieldwork of my own – preferably on nature conservation in another part of the world. This seemed an exciting and worthwhile field, though appointments and opportunities were bound to be rare – everyone I knew wanted a job just like that.

Turning over in my mind the few possibilities I'd heard of, I ran into Dr Fred Kurt, a staff member of the Game Research Department. We talked about jobs and he came up with a new and startling idea. 'Why don't you go to Sumatra?' he said. 'They want someone there to look after the orang utans.' Dr Kurt had spent three months of 1970 on a survey of rain forests in northern Sumatra, and was known for his enthusiasm about the place. Among the problems he had found there was the perilous situation of the orang utans which, though declining in numbers, were still being poached and sold on the black market. 'It might work', he said. 'I'll approach the Frankfurt Zoological Society about funds. There's another student – Regina Frey – interested too; you could join forces. You go and read some of the literature about orangs, and I'll put your name forward to work on the project.' I had met Regina, a younger student, from time to time in the course of our studies. We compared notes and ideas, and agreed that it all seemed very promising.

Orang utans are apes – close relatives of man – which were once widespread in the rain forests of south-east Asia. Even a brief survey of recent research showed their problem. The forests that are their only home are being cleared – both for timber and for agricultural development – at an ever-increasing rate. With their source of livelihood destroyed, orangs too are disappearing. In the whole island of Sumatra there are probably fewer than 5,000 left, confined entirely to the northern provinces where there are extensive forest reserves. Though protected by law throughout Indonesia, they have for many years been victims of a brisk trade – particularly the younger ones, which are easier to catch, handle and transport. Young orangs are popular pets and can sometimes be sold illicitly to collectors for zoos – though only the less reputable zoos buy orangs from the wild today.

Poachers are especially active around the reserves, where most orangs are to be found, and young animals are sometimes caught illegally during forestry operations or on farmland which replaces the cut-down forest. The conservation authorities often manage to seize young orangs from poachers and traders, but a seized animal still needs care and attention before it can be returned to the forest. Torn prematurely from its mother (for that is how most of them are caught), confined, mistreated, ill-fed and probably infected with parasites and disease, it stands little chance of survival without weeks or months of careful rehabilitation.

This problem was first recognized and tackled in the 1960s by Barbara Harrisson, who lived in Sarawak, North Borneo. Her idea was to set up a forest station where young apes, confiscated from illegal captivity by the authorities, could be systematically rehabilitated for life in the wild. This, she felt, would help to put an end to the illegal trade in orangs, for a rehabilitation centre would at last provide the conservation authorities with somewhere to take the orangs they had seized, as well as making it clear that conservation – not mere enforcement of the law – was the main objective. With Mrs Harrisson's help Sepilok, the first orang utan rehabilitation station, was set up in the Malaysian province of Sabah, North Borneo, in 1964.

Meanwhile the trade in orangs continued to flourish in South Borneo and Sumatra. So it was that in 1971, when the Dutch couple Herman and Ans Rijksen came to Sumatra to launch a field study on the behaviour of wild orangs, they decided to establish a local rehabilitation station at the same time. A little later a Canadian couple, Birouté and Ron Brindamour-Galdikas, followed their example in Kalimantan, the Indonesian part of Borneo.

Dr Kurt's plan was for us to start a second station of this kind in northern Sumatra, at some distance from the Rijksen's station though within the same great forest reserve. Neither Regina nor I had the least idea how it would all work out, but it all seemed an enticing prospect and we were willing to have a go.

5

There was one other big problem. How was I going to explain to my boyfriend, Markus, that I was trying to get to Sumatra for at least two years and possibly more? He too was just finishing a zoology course and looking for a job. Luckily this project in the rain-forest of far-off Sumatra fascinated him too. On the very next day he started enquiries of his own about opportunities for field studies abroad. To his delight he found there was a chance to work on problems connected with the protection of the Sumatran rhinoceros, another severely threatened species. This project, like my own, was short on planning and finance, and needed a lot of thought and hard work to make it viable. So we lunged together into the preliminaries, working out full proposals of what we wanted to do and writing to possible sponsors.

Markus succeeded in raising some of the money needed for the first year's work on rhinos. Then he approached the World Wildlife Fund International, in Morges, Switzerland, who took him on for a trial period as scientific assistant, giving him a three-months' practical course. After this the Fund agreed to bear the costs of the rest of his project, so Markus's work was secure. I made slower progress. Dr Kurt's approach to Frankfurt Zoological Society had already ensured most of the support needed, and later the World Wildlife Fund gave me its backing too. By midsummer 1972 we were certain that both projects were on, and could plan for departure before the end of the year.

But first, I had to spend some time at Frankfurt Zoo, learning the practical side of working with apes. The first month I spent mainly in mucking out the cages of the ape house. When I had time to spare from this really quite heavy work, I watched the orangs, gorillas and chimpanzees through the bars, getting to know them as individuals and working out differences between them. Then for two months I worked in the animal nursery. Here were my first contacts with orangs – two females barely a year old and two cheeky young males of three years or so – together with two gorillas, one a year old and the other a baby of three months. I learnt for the first time what it was like to be clutched by small but powerful four-handed apes, how to come to terms with them, and feed and look after them. These first encounters made me all the more eager to finish my apprenticeship and start working with orangs in the wild.

It was November 1972 when Markus and I finally set off for Sumatra. Regina, who had not yet finished her course, was to follow us six months later. To save money we travelled on the cheap – from Zurich to Calais in an unheated third-class carriage, then by ferry to Dover and finally to London. We arrived in London at nine o'clock in the morning of a bitterly cold but bright winter's day. With six hours to wait for our flight to Kuala Lumpur, and exhausted from the long freezing night, we had little enthusiasm for seeing the sights. Instead we warmed up in a café and ate two splendid English breakfasts apiece.

On the plane we were packed like sardines, but with only one stop-over the flight passed uneventfully. We reached Kuala Lumpur at 4 p.m. the following day, and were due to fly on to Jakarta, the capital of Indonesia, after a short break. But for ten weary hours a technical fault grounded the aircraft. Through the night and early hours of the morning we sat in the great open hall of the air terminal, drunk with exhaustion and almost gasping for breath in the warm, moisture-ladened air of the tropics. A riot of plant life surrounded and seemed to invade the hall – our first encounter with the exuberance of tropical vegetation. We dozed in a huddle on hard airport benches.

Jakarta itself was even hotter and more humid; getting out of the aircraft seemed like walking into a wall of warm cotton wool. Mr Sugito, an Indonesian nature conservation official, was waiting to meet us. Having slept away the 10 hours delay in his jeep at the airport, he drove us cheerfully to his headquarters at Bogor, about 50 miles from Jakarta. This was the main office of *Dinas Perlindungan dan Pengawetan Alam*, the Indonesian conservation authority to which we were responsible;

like everyone else we came to know it as the *Dinas* PPA, or just the PPA. Clucking hens running from under the wheels, white zebu oxen drawing two-wheeled carts, lively brown folk in colourful sarongs – we saw Indonesia as if in a dream, still too hot and exhausted to take it in. After introducing us to colleagues in the office, Mr Sugito took us to a small house in the country where we were to live for a few days. He had hardly disappeared when we staggered into the bedroom, collapsed across the bed and slept the whole day through.

In both our projects we were to work with the PPA, providing them with data, information and reports. For their part they would help us through the maze of red tape that surrounds anyone – especially foreigners – travelling and working in Indonesia, and give us the support of their staff in the field. Our first task was to exchange our tourist visas for visitors' visas, valid for several months. Next came a dull round of officialdom – from the police to the Council of Sciences, to the Forestry Commission and back to the police, filling in endless forms and distributing passport-sized photographs like confetti. After two weeks we finally had all the permits we needed, and the important official stamps in our passports. In fact it was a fortnight well spent, giving us time to acclimatize, slow down, adjust to Indonesian ways, and start to make ourselves at home in day-to-day life of the country.

Then we took off for Sumatra. After a two-hour flight we touched down in Medan, a city of over a million inhabitants and the provincial capital of northern Sumatra. We were met by Mr Bangun, head of the PPA in the province, who drove up in a dark green Toyota Landcruiser marked with the familiar panda motif of the World Wildlife Fund. Mr Bangun seemed morose and rather forbidding at first, but proved better for knowing. Through the ensuing months he shared our adventures and enthusiasms and helped us in many different ways, proving a dozen times over his own deep interest in the wildlife which PPA protected. The Toyota, he explained as we drove, had been presented by the WWF to help him step up inspection of the forest reserve boundaries. Still delighted with his new acquisition, he often drove it himself while his official driver rode as a passenger.

Now we were heading for Ketambe to meet the Rijksens, the Dutch couple who were already studying and rehabilitating orangs in the Alas valley. They too were working in co-operation with the World Wildlife Fund, and had invited us to spend the first few weeks with them. It was a long drive, taking the best part of a day, but it introduced us to the incredible variety of scenery and landscape to be found in northern Sumatra. To start with the road was tarmac-covered and ran through fairly flat country; cattle grazed in the fields and long-legged chickens foraged on the broad strips of grass flanking the road. Then steeper and steeper bends led us toward the mountains, from cultivated land into cloud forest with soaring trees, squat tree-ferns and dense undergrowth. Here at cloud level the vegetation grew rank and luxuriant, with mosses, creepers and shaggy plaits of lichens adorning the trees and rocks.

At the top of a ridge we found a little town – Berastagi – whose cool climate makes it a holiday resort for town-dwellers and tourists, as well as the centre of North Sumatra's most fertile market gardening area. Along the main street were market stalls with heaps of strange, exotic fruits; behind them, no less colourful and curious to the strangers passing through, stood the local Karo women with their bright dresses and dark red turban-like headcloths. Now the road quickly deteriorated. There was no more tarmac – the highway became a succession of boulders, ruts and shingle patches, varied by the remains of landslides washed down from the hillsides above.

For several hours longer we bounced through highlands cleared of forest and bare as steppes – the sad consequence of ruthless timber-felling and slash-and-burn agriculture – finally reaching the valley of the river Alas. This is a broad, fertile valley, patterned like a patchwork quilt with *sawahs* (paddy fields) criss-crossed by lines of coconut palms and dotted with tiny settlements. Beyond the valley loomed the range of high, timber-covered mountains that form the Gunung Leuser Reserve – part of the great complex of forest reserves filling the heartland of northern Sumatra, and providing the home for most of its remaining orang-utans.

At Kotacane, the valley's biggest village, we stopped for a rest and a breather. With inquisitive children crowding around Mr Bangun, the driver and Markus and I found a tiny roadside café, where we ordered successive glasses of hot, sweet tea. Far more refreshing than cold drinks, it laid the dust and finally quenched our raging thirsts. The more we drank, the more we sweated, until it seemed as though the tea was running in through our mouths and straight out through our pores. Then back into the Toyota and on for the last leg of the journey. For 1½ hours we ran alongside the river, on a shingle flood-plain crossed by a succession of side-streams. The road was punctuated by water-filled ruts and potholes whose depth we found out the hard way. Bridges – such as there were – had fallen into decrepitude long before and no-one had dreamed of mending or replacing them. Mr Bangun explained that the locals re-arranged the boulders in the stream-beds from time to time, making what was poetically known as a *jalan air* or 'water road'. Over these water roads the Toyota staggered indomitably, ploughing through shingle banks and crossing rapids with axles and floorboards awash. Occasionally we laid planks over the gaps in ruined bridges, standing clear while the driver wobbled over them like a tight-rope walker.

As evening drew in we reached our destination. Ketambe station lies across the Alas river, which at this point forms the eastern boundary of the Gunung Leuser Reserve. With the rains already started the river was in spate – a torrent of muddy brown water 130 feet across, full of branches broken with tumbling waves. Jaded by the long journey, my spirit of adventure sank to zero. But a *perahu* or dug-out canoe stood waiting, manned by wiry Indonesian boatmen who seemed to know exactly what to do. Our luggage was loaded aboard and we squatted one behind the other in the bottom of the canoe, clinging to both sides. 'Just sit still, even if the boat starts rocking,' said Mr Bangun, 'otherwise we'll capsize for sure.' He added in passing that he couldn't swim, but didn't seem unduly perturbed by the strength of the current or the frailty of our boat.

In fact it was all too easy. Swiftly and surely the boatmen poled the canoe across the river, landing us about 30 yards downstream in the Gunung Leuser Reserve. Herman and Ans Rijksen were there to welcome us and take us the few extra yards to their station. We spent the evening in a cosy wooden bungalow with palm-leaf roof, getting to know them and talking over a supper that lasted far into the night. Later, lying in our camp beds, almost too tired to sleep, we listened to the chirping of the crickets and the quiet, soft whispers of the jungle. It was then, I think, we realised that the adventure we had planned for so long was happening – it was with us, and just about to begin in earnest.

2
Into the Forest

Next morning Herman took us on our first walk in the forest.
His research zone had a network of cleared paths, so we could
make our way without effort. Soon we were wrapped in the
jungle's humid, earthy scent and entranced by its palette of
dark greens and browns. Clusters of young leaves, hanging
limp and still from their stalks, had an early-morning transpa-
rency about them – even an unexpected shimmer of bright red
in the clear sunlight. Climbing plants and creepers covered
every trunk, festooned from branches like curtains. Here and
there they combined with spiders' webs and strong young
shoots to form an almost impenetrable wall, which Herman cut
with his jungle knife.

Slipping through the gaps, we scrambled over fallen trees
already overgrown and rotting, and crept under sodden trunks
dripping with fungi and moss. It was quiet in the forest – only
the incessant, unvarying song of the cicadas and the occasional
snap of a branch under our feet broke the morning stillness. Yet
we had the feeling of being surrounded and engulfed by a vast
profusion of living creatures – all alert to us, watching and
scenting us, moving away as we advanced and closing in silently
behind. There was no feeling of hostility – just an acceptance
that we were there; the forest was keeping an eye on us.

Suddenly something bit me in the calf – a sharp nip that really
was hostile. I carefully rolled up the leg of my slacks, and there

hung a leech, 2 inches long and firmly attached by suckers at both ends. Happily drinking my blood through a tiny puncture wound, it held on tightly, so slippery that I could scarcely tear it off. Finally I pulled it free, but it straight away attached itself to my fingers, and proved just as difficult to shift again. So I cut it bloodily with my knife and managed to throw it away. This was the first of many encounters with leeches. As time went on we learned to deal with them more effectively, rolling them into a ball with a quick movement of thumb and forefinger and flicking them nonchalantly away. But to start with they were disconcerting, and very impressive in their efficiency at finding prey.

As a zoologist I was fascinated by them. They stood upright on the vegetation, waving long, threadlike bodies to and fro. Warmth, smell or vibrations tell them that prey is coming, and they move like looper caterpillars unerringly toward their target. Landing on trousers, shirts or shoes, they find a gap and get at the bare skin; the bites don't hurt much and are not poisonous – less painful indeed than the bites of mosquitoes or horseflies, which also abounded in the forest. Leeches feed to repletion, then drop off quietly to digest their meal and wait – perhaps several months – for their next one.

Our circular tour in the research area lasted about three hours. At the end of it a surprise bonus awaited us – a family of gibbons swinging its way from branch to branch above our heads. With alternating circular sweeps of their arms they swung from one tree to the next, as fast and light as birds in flight. Even more like birds, the adults were singing a light-hearted duet, the female calling with a rising scale and the males falling in with a twitter at the end.

After 18 months in Sumatra the Rijksens were ready for home leave. Disappearing for 2 months to the Netherlands, they kindly offered us the run of Ketambe station while they were away. This gave Markus and me a chance to familiarise ourselves gradually with the tropics, the forest and our animals.

From the staff of the station we learnt our first halting phrases of Indonesian. While I got to know the fifteen or more orangs on the station and discovered how to tell them apart, Markus made himself known to local villagers who might help with his travelling. He also took lessons in throwing the *jala*. This is a circular net, attached at its centre to a cord, with a chain of weights around the edge. You throw it so that it lands spread out on the water; then the heavy edge sinks rapidly to the bottom. The fish, scared by the splash, swim upward into the middle and are caught by the mesh. Fishermen used them on all the local rivers; they could well provide food for Markus and his guides and bearers on their travels in search of rhinoceros.

It was not long before Markus started preparing for his first expedition into the depths of the Reserve. He went round the villages buying up cooking pots, plastic sheeting, rice and dried fish, and hired a few bearers and a guide. This sortie was to last only two weeks; Markus just wanted to learn how to travel in the reserve, to live in the forest and get along with the Indonesians. So I stayed alone back at the station, keeping up its routine and learning about orangs and their forest background.

The river was a constant delight. Big round stones were scattered along its banks, and in the evening when I bathed a troop of monkeys – crab-eating macaques – often paraded along the other side. The locals called them *kera*, after their croaking call. Sometimes I heard an otter's whistle and crept round a bend in the stream to see its fresh footprints in the sand. Twice I managed to watch a pair of these charming trick swimmers and divers. Their heads seemed to skip through the waves, disappearing and then popping up again a few yards downstream. Their big mouths were surrounded with prickly whiskers which glinted in the evening sun. They gave happy whistles and vanished among the ripples.

In the evenings Pak Amansar sometimes looked in on me. The station foreman, he was a wise old man and a delightful conversationalist. He came from the Gayo tribe, so he said, a group which has its home in the northern Alas valley and the mountains around. Pak Amansar reckoned that I was not learning Indonesian fast enough, and did his best to help. So he came to visit me again and again to tell me long stories. He could not speak English, but often had to frame a sentence in several different ways until, struggling with my dictionary, I grasped what he was trying to say. He was persistent and kind, and slowly I began to make progress.

'*Kapan Tuan Markus akan kembali dari hutan?*' – 'When is Markus coming back from the forest?' he would ask me practically every day. He was worried about having to bear sole responsibility for a helpless woman like me. Every evening he made the rounds of my house to check that all the doors were bolted.

But daytime belonged to the orangs. I spent hours at the station watching them – both the free-living animals on their way to rehabilitation and occasional wild visitors – as they climbed about, chewed leaves or played near the feeding place. Gradually I got to know them as individuals, discovering the differences in character and temperament that gave them their individuality. I learnt how to build cages, and helped the station staff at feeding time, trying all the while to get a feel for the problems of rehabilitating orang utans, and the best ways of tackling them. The weeks at Ketambe were invaluable experience toward running my own station. After long talks with Herman before he went away, and long days of observation on the station itself, I began to feel that I knew how to go about setting up a similar enterprise, making as few mistakes as possible.

Hours spent deep in the forest were invaluable too. Not far from Ketambe were huge tracts of almost undisturbed rain forest, where I could wander alone for hours on end seeking wild orangs. They were not always easy to find. Unlike most other monkeys and apes, orangs tend to be solitary creatures, living alone or in small family groups of two or three. There are seldom more than one or two animals per square kilometer (roughly 250 acres) of forest. But placid in temperament, and not readily scared, they rarely take fright and are comparatively easy to watch. Once I found them, I could often stay with a group for the rest of the day, and sometimes return in the morning to find them again in the same small area.

Until a few years ago practically nothing was known of the orang-utan's way of life. It was only in the late 1960s that a few individual workers set about studying them in the wild; notable among them were David Horr, the Rodmans, John MacKinnon, and more recently Herman Rijksen and Birouté Brindamour-Galdikas. We still have much to learn about these gentle apes. Orangs do not have well marked-out territories, to be defended in skirmishes with fellow members of the species. Instead they seem to keep to overlapping home ranges. Compared with wandering at random, home ranges have the advantage of allowing the apes to become thoroughly familiar with an extensive piece of forest, so they can learn the best routes through the canopy, and know where to find the best food trees at different times of the year.

They live almost entirely in the trees, well away from the wet, muddy ground of the forest floor, feeding mainly on the variety of fruits that the rain forest provides throughout most of the year. Moving around from tree-top to tree-top they take different fruits as they ripen. Happening upon a richly ladened tree, they may spend several days there, feasting steadily. Frequently the hornbill shows them the way to these banquets; his loud croaking and the whistling beat of his wings can be heard a long way off.

Between gorging themselves on fruit, orangs eat young shoots and leaves and gnaw at bark, or pull branches apart to get at the soft medulla inside. They chew lianas – the slender hanging trunks of climbing plants – and are also partly car-

16

Overleaf: Mehra. *Above:* Building a nest. This young wild orang sits on a bough pulling smaller branches towards him and treading them into place.

Fully-grown male orang climbing a liana. The moon-shape face is characteristic of adult males.

Olip

Above left: Five-year-old female. *Above right:* Pesek. *Below:* Nakal and Murka.

A young male sitting on a fallen tree. The long shoulder-fur acts as a cape, helping to keep off the rain.

This young orang holds onto a branch with one hand and a foot while thoughtfully scratching his other foot with his open hand. *Overleaf:* One of the smallest rehabilitation patients.

nivorous: they delight in picking termites out of crevices with their lips and fingers. They also like to raid ants' nests, and they find beetles and grasshoppers another nice change. They are unlikely to turn up their noses at a clutch of birds' eggs, should they find one, but are not known to eat small birds or mammals – except possibly as an occasional experiment.

Social organization among orangs is not really clear. John MacKinnon, who has studied orangs in Borneo and Sumatra (chapter 4), sees it as the clumping of a number of 'sub-groups' – lone males or females, mothers with one or two young, occasional male and female pairs, and other small combinations – around single dominant adult males. So a group may consist of a dozen or more animals, all known to each other and frequently meeting, but generally circulating in their sub-groups around the patriarch. Sub-groups often meet in their wanderings through the forest, but the meetings are usually peaceable; fights and even serious threatening behaviour seem to be very rare among orangs. There are occasions when several animals meet in the same small area without hostility. If the fruit of a particular tree – durian, for example – ripens all at once and it is a favourite fruit of orangs, several sub-groups of orangs may converge upon it and feed together. When this happens there is clear evidence of a hierarchy among them – a pecking-order known to each individual but scarcely apparent except in these circumstances. Old-man orangs rank highest, followed by adult females and then by the lower ranks in strict order. But gatherings of this kind are rare. Generally orangs seem to prefer to go on their own way, on friendly nodding terms with the rest of their group but living and foraging alone. Only mothers with infants, young animals and those ready to mate seek the close company of another orang.

The rain forest and its climate have made the orang what he is today, providing him with all he needs for his quiet, peaceable existence. The tall, closely-packed trees and lianas, whose tops form two or three separate storeys of leaves, give him scope for

17

his skills in climbing and an easy way of getting about. The hot, humid climate varies little with the seasons, so that trees in fruit and young shoots and leaves are ready for eating practically all the year round. Orangs can always find a table laid for them somewhere in the forest, though it may not be laid in abundance; a single tree may carry enough fruit for two or three orangs, but only exceptionally enough for a dozen. And they may have to travel long distances from one table to the next, for the nearest tree of the same species with fruit ready ripened may be several miles away. Hence their solitary or semi-solitary existence and their nomadic home-is-where-you-make-it lifestyle.

In most people's minds the tropical rain forest evokes an image of boundless fertility. But it is the variety of animal and plant life, as well as the exuberance, that characterises this environment. Some 3,000 different species of tree are to be found on the Indonesian Islands; the whole of central Europe has only 36 species. On the trunks and branches of all the trees are dozens of ferns, orchids and other epiphytes – sometimes as many as 50 species on the same tree. In Indonesia alone over 20,000 different kinds of flowering plants have been identified. With its multiplicity of species, the tropical rain forest is an ocean of hereditary material, offering almost inexhaustible possibilities for the formation of new species.

Whatever falls to the ground in the rain forest – leaves, fruit, tree trunks or animals – is rapidly broken up and decomposed by countless micro-organisms. Their level of activity is higher than in temperate regions, because of the prevailing warmth and moisture; so minerals from the fallen material are straightaway released to the soil and taken up again by the roots of the plants. Thus almost all of the organic material of these forests is to be found circulating within the plants themselves, and very little of it in the soil. The layer of humus may be no more than 3 or 4 inches thick, so that even an elephant's footprint can lay bare the infertile clay sub-soil beneath. Only the continuous canopy of leaves, helped by the lower layers of vegetation, prevent the all-important humus from being washed away by the daily heavy rainfall.

The forest reserves of northern Sumatra are only a tiny remnant of the vast, continuous rain forest that once clothed virtually the whole of the island. Destruction has been a gradual process, accelerating rapidly in recent years with increasing pressure from the human population and increasing demand from the world outside for tropical hardwood timbers. At present about 130 million people live on Indonesia's innumerable islands. In thirty years the figure may well be doubled. As the population grows, and demands for higher standards of living increase, more and more of the forest is destroyed to provide both room and capital benefits. Following oil, timber from the rain forest is Indonesia's second most important export and source of foreign currency. In 1967 just over half a million cubic metres of wood were exported; by 1971 this had increased to 15 million cubic metres, and demand was growing steadily. The wood is sold to Japan, Europe and USA, some of it for high quality building timbers and veneers, but mostly to make paper.

Once destroyed, the rain forest cannot be replanted. It would be impossible to re-establish artificially the enormous variety of species. The only other technique for exploiting the forest, that keeps it intact and allows it to regenerate, is the selective culling of the largest trees. If this is done properly, with conservation as one of the objectives, the forest has a chance to restore itself over a period of 20 to 50 years, when the largest trunks can again be taken. Timber companies with long-term concessions have followed systems of this kind since the 1950s, reaping a steady income from the forest without destroying it. But unfortunately, contractors with shorter-term interests do not bother about forestry laws. Quick returns by illegal clear felling are their sole aim; they reduce costs by exporting as much as possible as quickly as possible. So huge areas of rain forest fall to the chain saw; the timber floats down the rivers or trundles across country on lorries for export, and the ground lies open and unprotected.

Left to itself, selectively-logged forest land may still recover if the undergrowth has time and opportunity to regenerate, and act as a nursery for the larger trees. But here another factor steps in. Besides cutting down trees, timber companies open up roads into the forest, and these are often responsible for the final stage of devastation. In their efforts to bring more land into production, nearby farmers push forward along the roads into the opened-up sections of forest, clearing large areas of the remaining brush by burning. Stripped of the last of its cover, the soil is now open to the skies and completely at the mercy of rain and wind. The meagre covering of humus quickly erodes away, its departure speeded by the disturbance of cultivation.

Deforested ground in an upland area of high rainfall can sometimes be farmed for two or three profitable seasons, but seldom for longer. The initial bonus of minerals gained from burning the under-brush soon leaches away. What is left is a barren wasteland of sterile soil and clay, useless alike to man, plant or beast. But the real tragedy of this whole unhappy business is that the final phase of destruction – is completely unnecessary. Of Sumatra's 186,000 square miles, almost 40 per cent is potentially good agricultural land, much of it in the lowlands and currently lying fallow, barren and uncultivated. With suitable irrigation schemes and sensible use of fertilizers, plantations and paddy fields could be established in these areas, providing far more extra food per acre – on a permanent basis – than all the bare, wasted uplands of devastated forests.

Rain forests are in many ways essential to the human population. They hold on to the rainfall like a sponge, releasing it gradually between storms. Flooding generally occurs only where the forest has been stripped and the torrential rains can no longer be contained. Again, since the forest constantly evaporates water back into the atmosphere, there is never a lack of regular rainfall – on which both forest and crops depend. Once forests have been destroyed, there is a strong chance of complete climatic change, floods alternating with drought to the ultimate destruction of all human effort in the area.

The human population of Indonesia depends on the survival of the forest remnants. Even more dependent are the original forest dwellers – orang-utans, gibbons, siamangs, rhinoceroses and clouded leopards, to name but a few – that evolved over millions of years to live in tropical rain forest and have no chance of survival when it is gone.

As many of the orangs I would handle for rehabilitation were likely to be youngsters, often torn prematurely from contact with their mothers, I was especially interested in studying family life at Ketambe – watching the interactions between parents and young and the gradual development of independence in juveniles.

Adult male orangs are usually solitary and play no part in rearing the young. Adult females nearly always have with them one or more young, occasionally with a sub-adult male in attendance. Females are interested in pairing only during a brief spell between pregnancies, when several males may show interest in them for a few days or weeks at a time. After mating, and a pregnancy lasting about 9 months, the female gives birth to a tiny baby weighing about 3 pounds. During its first 5 or 6 months the baby clings day and night to its mother's furry coat. She may give it additional support, but its four-handed grip is usually enough, leaving her hands free for climbing. At 4 to 6 months it begins to embark on small excursions of its own, always keeping close enough to its mother to be able to hang on again quickly.

The young stay with their mother and share her nests for as long as they remain dependent on her – usually 3 to 4 years at least. Nest building, like so many other facets of their behaviour, is essentially innate but has to be practised; climbing too is an unborn skill that develops and elaborates during the first few years of life, and ability to seek out and discriminate food plants may be the same. Even at the age of 1 year, long before weaning, the young apes practise these skills regularly. They begin to play with small branches and weave them into tiny nests, throw themselves into difficult positions among the branches and extricate themselves again with increasingly coordinated limb movements, and feed on the plants their mother feeds on.

During these first few years, when so much is being learnt, a mother's presence is no less important to young orangs than it is to human children. Where humans usually live in family groups with fathers, brothers and sisters to play with – often grannies, aunts and cousins as well – baby orangs have only their mother. She must be a constant companion, a playmate, a refuge, and a shining example of all the skills; if she is not present, there is no substitute or understudy to take her place in the infant's life.

A young orang seldom finds others of its own age to play with. So it invents a whole series of games with branches, leaves and other materials, that it can play by itself. It drapes carefully-woven leafy twigs like a victor's laurels around its neck, or finds the most complicated way of balancing a branch on its shoulders or head. It builds small play-nests, or tears an old, dried-out nest to pieces, watching the leaves and twigs fall rustling to the ground. Its gymnastics are limitless, trapezing on lianas, testing the springiness of branches, and racing hand over hand up vertical stems. Now and then it may wheedle its mother into a wrestling match, but most of its play is solitary.

Young orangs often stay on with their mothers for a while after the next baby is born. They may share the nest with her and the baby, and sometimes let themselves be carried. When this happens, the tiny infant clings to one side of its mother and the older one to the other side. By being together with mother and baby, a young female orang probably aquires useful experience that will stand it in good stead when the time comes for it to rear offspring of its own. A little later, half grown and close to independence, the youngster gradually drifts away from its mother's side and wanders on its own, finally taking off into the forest as a young, independent sub-adult.

Female orangs that are pregnant or tending small babies show no interest in the attention of males. Only when their offspring are 3 years old or more, and well on the way to independence, does interest in the opposite sex begin to awaken. Because orang males so rarely find a female just ready to accept them, many start accompanying mothers with young long before the critical period of ovulation and heat. As the infant matures, the escort is gradually accepted as a companion by the mother, and stands a good chance of mating when she comes on heat. Or they remain with females through pregnancy, staying with them until after the baby is born. In these family groups, referred to by John MacKinnon as 'consort pairs', the males are most often young adults. As they grow older they are less likely to pair in this way; at ages between 16 and 20, when they are fully grown, they tend more and more to be loners – the patriarchs around which the sub-groups of younger orangs gravitate.

I watched the behaviour of a mother-with-young in the company of a consort male, one day toward the end of my stay at Ketambe. The mother and her baby I had followed for several hours the day before, seeing them settle into their nest in the evening. Next morning I returned at first light, just in time to watch them awaken and move from the nest. To my surprise they were no longer alone. A young male, still not fully grown but sporting a jaunty blond beard, moved off through the trees with them. He must have spent the night nearby, though I had not spotted his nest in the fading light the evening before. He and the female seemed to know each other and be on good terms, sitting side by side without signs of anxiety or aggression.

The infant, less sure of the newcomer, hid cautiously behind

23

its mother. Every now and again it would make an angry attack on the male, hanging with three hands to its mother's side and swinging at him with the fourth, baring its teeth in a soundless grimace of rage. Then a moment later it withdrew nervously to the shelter of its mother's back. The male took no notice at all of this childish provocation. Maybe he was the father; there was no way of telling, though the mother and he were old aquaintances, pleasantly relaxed in each others' company. They moved together all through the morning, feeding on the same trees and keeping in sight of each other the whole time.

In the late afternoon the rain clouds gathered as usual, and heavy drops of rain began to fall. The leaves around me flipped and rattled under their impact. The infant orang and its mother withdrew from the open branches to a sheltered spot under a dense canopy, but the young male, like me, continued to squat indolently where he was. He broke off a branch thick with leaves and held it over his head with one hand. At the same time he curled up into a red ball of fur, drawing in arms, legs and head so as to offer the smallest body surface to the rain. From under his umbrella of foliage he glared out balefully at the dripping leaves. The rain ran down his wiry, greasy hair, which acted as a raincoat, getting wet only at the tips and keeping most of the rain off his skin.

After a few minutes of downpour the shower gradually eased. I was wet through, but the rain was warm and didn't worry me. The male orang too seemed quite happy. Still curled up with the leaf umbrella over his head, he was stretching out his lower lip to catch the trickles of water running off the leaves. Mother and infant too still sat under their shelter. With a loud smacking of lips the infant was sucking water off one of his legs, which had remained outside the shelter and caught some of the rain. Having partly dried his leg, he drew it up and squeezed it against his body, extending the other one in its place.

But suddenly his patience ran out and a burst of energy overtook him. Hauling himself up by his right arm and leg, he swung himself hard against his mother, giving her what might have been an intentional come-and-play-with-me knock. She bared her teeth, drawing her lips back in a friendly grin; then with a chuckle of laughter she let herself be drawn into the game. Grasping her offspring in both hands, she pulled him onto her lap and bent over him, playfully nibbling his foot.

I left them to their game and made my way home through the dripping forest.

3
Lake Bangko Journey

Watching and learning took up most of my time at Ketambe,
but there were other things to do as well. Between whiles I
started to sketch out plans for the living quarters and cages of
the new station. Like Ketambe, there had to be separate
quarantine and rehabilitation cages for the orangs, and we
needed two separate houses, one for Regina and me and the
other for the staff. It seemed best for the Indonesian staff and us
each to have our own quarters, where we could follow our own
slightly different patterns of life without imposing on each
other and getting in each other's hair. So I planned for two
houses, one with two bedrooms, a terrace, a bathroom and a
kitchen for Regina and me, and the other with one big living
and sleeping room, a terrace and a kitchen for the staff. Both
were to be on stilts to protect them from damp, and we wanted
them built in the local style with walls of boarding and a roof
thatch of palm leaves.

Markus surfaced from his first expedition in the middle of
the night. Soaked in sweat, he was dripping wet and caked with
mud, and his hands were scratched to pieces by rattan thorns.
But he'd had a wonderful trip and radiated enthusiasm.

'Do you know what we saw?' he said 'You'd never guess – an
elephant! Right close too – I got a photograph of him!' And he
told me the story of how, at the edge of a stream, they had found
the big fresh footprints, and followed them until the stream

wound away into a deep forested gorge. As they came round a bend they suddenly saw the grey giant before them, about 100 feet away. Markus was fascinated and saw the chance – perhaps his only chance ever – of a good photograph. The others of his party were less enthusiastic, so Markus crawled on alone, stalking his elephant with camera poised. As he pressed the trigger the elephant turned towards him. Chewing a young banana stem, it spread its big ears to pinpoint the sound of the intruder and began to look faintly hostile. Markus's party turned and fled. Markus ran too, plunging, slipping and stumbling over the wet stones and feeling very vulnerable and small. He realized as he ran that the sides of the stream were almost vertical rock walls; if the elephant decided to charge, the stream bed was the only possible way out. But the elephant turned his ears the other way and continued munching his banana stem.

'It was enormous!' raved Markus, spreading his hands like a fisherman. 'You'll see it on the photo.' Big or small, wild elephants are rare in Sumatra these days and we looked forward to seeing this one when the pictures came back. But sadly, the elephant looked tiny and very far away, difficult to see among the dense vegetation and nothing like the giant it had appeared in the stream valley. It was one of the few that either of us saw, though we often used well-worn elephant tracks in our wanderings about the forests.

However, Markus had found out a lot on his first trip and gained useful experience in the forest. Now he was keen to go further, with a longer expedition to a remote area where he hoped his rare Sumatran rhino might be found. He was off again shortly, and I stayed at the station on my own, continuing my observations on both captive and wild orangs.

In mid-February the Rijksens returned from their home leave. A few days later, when Markus came back from his second trip, we decided on a joint excursion over to the west coast of Aceh, taking in the northern end of the island. The province of Aceh forms the northernmost tip of Sumatra, and its steep mountains and valleys have for long made it remote and inaccessible. The people there are quite different from those of the south, highly traditional, with a long history of freedom and independence from the rest of the island. In the seventeenth century Aceh was an independent sultanate with a rich economy of its own, involving working elephants from India and slaves. It was the end of the eighteenth century before the Dutch colonisers took it over, long after the rest of Sumatra had succumbed, and even then resistance continued for two decades or more. In many parts of Aceh whites of any nation are today liable to hear shouts of *'Belanda'* (Dutchman), still a term of abuse hurled in memory of the conquest.

The aim of the trip was to look for a site for our own rehabilitation station on the west coast of Aceh. Almost two-thirds of the Sumatran orangs that were finding their unhappy way onto the black market seemed to be coming from this far-distant, inaccessible area of the north and west, so both the Rijksens and I had good reasons for having a look at it. A rehabilitation station there would be fully justified. Orangs seized locally by the authorities would not have to travel so far for rehabilitation, and the station would provide a centre from which poaching and trading could be monitored, and possibly reduced.

From the map we had chosen the Kluet Reserve as a possible site. This reserve, the smallest and western-most of the three forest reserves, forms a salient about 20 miles wide adjoining the much bigger Gunung Leuser Reserve. It runs down from the mountains to the low ground and marshy forests of the littoral, with a wide range of natural habitats including a small lake. To north and south the Kluet Reserve is bounded by rivers, and the lake – Danau Bangko – lies almost in the middle. That was where we were heading for in the Rijksen's heavily loaded Toyota, one morning early in March.

Though Danau Bangko lay south and west of Ketambe, several ranges of impassable mountains stood between. We had to drive south and eastward to Medan (along the abysmal road I have already described), then head north and west to Banda Aceh, the capital of the privince which stands at the northern tip of the island. Then the road led southward down the west coast to Tapaktuan, coming to an end in villages scattered about the area. It would take 35 to 40 hours' driving – about 5 days' travelling altogether.

We made slow progress, for the roads were uniformly bad – muddy and full of deep potholes, and nowhere near so impressive as they appeared on the maps. But the scenery was wonderfully varied. Low groves of nipa palms, covering large areas of swamp and mud-flat, alternated with hilly pasture-land not unlike the foothills of our own Swiss Alps. Then the road turned to sand as it ran along a picture-book coastline, with fishing villages and groves of coconut palms. Mazes of fishing nets were hung up to dry among the palms. We ate and slept in little restaurants and inns along the road.

On the evening of the fifth day we were in Tapaktuan, meeting the local PPA representative, Gersom Sinaga. Next morning we set off, with Gersom as guide, for the edge of the Kluet Reserve. Here the boggy, forest-covered lowlands stretched right down to the sandy shore of the Indian Ocean. The hothouse climate and the hordes of bloodthirsty insects were horrifying, but the variety and luxuriance of the vegetation made up for a great deal of our discomfort. We'd never seen anything remotely like it before, and were fascinated.

At a tiny village by the end of a track we hired four small *perahus* (dug-out canoes), whose owners agreed to take us the rest of the way by water to Lake Bangko. Herman and Ans sat in one boat, while Markus accompanied Gersom Sinaga in the second. I sat in the third, squatting comfortably cross-legged on the pile of luggage, and the fourth took the rest of our equipment. We brought with us tents, sleeping bags, cooking kit, rice, and a change of clothes. To start with the boatmen poled the long, narrow canoes upstream. When they grounded in the shallows the men got out and, standing up to their waist in water, pushed the canoes until they floated again. But soon the stream grew narrower and shallower, and lost itself altogether in the marshy vegetation. We dragged the canoes forward by tugging with our hands at the tall grass tussocks on either side, stirring up clouds of insects at every yard.

Now the marsh and water meadows gave way to rolling woodlands. This was by far the hardest section of the route. Again and again our way was blocked by thickets of thorny undergrowth and fallen trees. We had to get out and walk, the men joining forces to carry the heavy canoes – even heavier with the luggage in them – over one obstacle after another. In the evening we pitched camp. After a dip in the peaty brown waters of the stream we gorged ourselves on what I was coming to recognize as the standard Indonesian camping ration – dried fish, fried in oil and served with mountains of boiled rice. However unattractive it may sound, it was sensible food, easily prepared and just right for the end of a hot, hard day's travel. We washed it down with pints of hot tea which, in the circumstances, were as welcome as any more exotic drink we could imagine.

Markus and I shared a tiny low tent with no windows – admirable, we thought, for keeping out the swarms of mosquitoes and other biting flies. So it was, but it turned out to be practically airtight as well, with little or no ventilation. When I awoke in the night my hair, clothes, sleeping bag and everything else were dripping wet; it wasn't raining, but the moisture of the warm air inside the tent was condensing on the cool walls and running down to soak us. We opened the tent door briefly, but hungry hordes of mosquitoes swarmed in and settled on us they had apparently been waiting outside for just such an opportunity. So we spent the rest of the night soaked through and actually shivering. We got up much too early and stumbled crossly about the camp until the others awoke and we could unpack the dry clothes.

That morning we continued to follow the boggy trickle that the stream had become. Around midday it started to widen as we approached the foot of the lake. We glided through forest, between the pillars and arches formed by roots of giant fig trees, through a maze of arched tunnels; we weaved our way through bamboos and pandanas, with tufts of grassy leaves soaring far above our heads on either side. Suddenly the stream widened, giving us a breathtaking view of the still, dark lake, smooth as a mirror, and framed in hills of virgin forest. We paddled eagerly across, to where our guides knew of an abandoned fishermen's camp on the far side.

'Are there crocodiles here?' I wanted to know. 'Yes of course three small ones and one big', said one of the boatmen. I'm not sure where the information came from or how accurate it was, but Lake Bangko *looked* like a paradise for crocodiles of all sizes.

At last we reached the shore, and disembarked to stretch cramped limbs. We had been looking forward to a good swim in the lake; the water was luke-warm, probably 30 °C at least, but would still be refreshing. But a glance at our escorts killed our enthusiasm stone-dead. With sarongs held high they had been dragging the boats up onto the bank; now their wet shins were decorated with giant leeches a good four inches long. 'Buffalo leeches', they called them cheerfully, and the water seemed to be swarming with plenty more. So we settled for a shower from the kitchen bucket and a gentle evening paddle over the lake. That night, as the forest all round gleamed softly in the moonlight, Lake Bangko was our very own.

But however beautiful and well situated, Lake Bangko was out of the question for a station. Though central to the Kluet Reserve, it was too remote, and far too difficult to get to from other centres. We needed good communications, both for supplies and to ensure that captive animals could be got to us without too much difficulty. And the climate of the swamp forest, with temperatures of 30°–32 °C and relative humidities of 90 per cent more, was something we would not have been able to live with for long.

For several more days we searched the Kluet Reserve in the hope of finding a better site, but without success. Certainly there were wild orangs here; we saw several recently-built nests, and once a young male swung away from us through the trees. But we had to admit that the area wasn't suitable. Quite apart from the transport and communication problems and the shocking climate, we were beginning to sense a degree of hostility from the very conservative local population. Their Mohammedan background and long tradition of xenophobia could make it very difficult for two strangers – especially two women – to work among them, on a project which they might well feel was alien and far removed from their own ways of life. We were conservationists, not missionaries, and needed a place where we could work more effectively.

However, this strange, remote region of the west coast provided us with our first five candidates for rehabilitation. Eating supper that night in Gersom Sinaga's home, we were visited by Pak Minim, a keen local colleague of Gersom's. He told us of a captive orang kept by a local forester in a village just south of the Kluet Reserve, a few miles down the track. Next morning Pak Minim guided us to the forester's house. We could see the orang from the road. It was climbing up and down a pillar which held up the lean-to roof in front of the house. A steel chain about five feet long, with one end fixed to the foot of the pillar, hung about the animal's neck. It was a 3 year-old female but looked much older, with the grey hair and wrinkled face of an old woman. All that remained of her original colour was a reddish tuft of fur on her belly. The owner, slightly apprehensive at our arrival, recovered quickly and claimed that he had seized the orang for the PPA; he even wanted compensation for the cost of its keep. But Gersom wasn't impressed – even to us it sounded a pretty thin story. Gersom bent down, cut the wire that fastened the chain, and carried off the little ape in his arms.

So we aquired Mania, our very first orang. On the way back to Gersom's she sat on my lap and gazed attentively through the windows with wise old eyes. We had no station as yet – not even a cage to put her in – but it was with Mania that our project finally achieved reality. I had come to Sumatra to rehabilitate orangs. Now I had one to rehabilitate.

I left Mania in Gersom's care, giving him money to pay for her keep, and for having her wormed and sent on to us when our station took shape. I also promised to pay all the costs of moving any other orangs that Gersom seized. He was delighted about this. 'There are lots of captive orangs here', he said, 'scattered about the villages and waiting for someone to put a price on them. Up to now I haven't had the resources to take possession of them, and feed and move them; if you can pay the bills, I'll start rounding them up tomorrow.'

And so he did. Shortly after we were back in Ketambe, Gersom wrote in to say he had seized another four orangs; he wanted to crate them up and shift them out to us as soon as possible. I was no nearer to finding the site for our station and simply could not cope with orangs at this stage. But Mr Bangun, our good friend in the PPA, came to our rescue with an empty cage in his garden at Medan. Gersom sent the five orangs to him, in a couple of crates on top of the Medan bus. He looked after them for the time being, while I continued my search for a place to build.

While the main threat to orangs is destruction of their habitat, hunting and trading still exert an additional strain on the stocks of animals remaining, as Gersom's round-up testified. Hunting is not a new problem. From the earliest days orangs have been taken for food. They were hunted by the natives of Sumatra and Borneo long before white men became aware of them. Stone Age remains from the Niah caves of Sarawak include charred orang bones 37,000 years old; most are from females and half-grown animals, suggesting that Stone Age man could not catch the more powerful adult males. However, the total impact of these early hunters on stocks of orangs can only have been slight. Hunting for the pot still occurs in some primitive corners of Indonesia today, though not everywhere; there are areas of Indonesia where orangs are thought to be inhabited by the souls of the dead, and not to be interfered with. Native lore often respects the orang's closeness to man, and generally helps to protect it.

Later orangs were killed for food or sport, or to protect crops. Though they normally live exclusively in rain forest, destruction of the forest for agriculture means they must seek alternatives. They may happily invade man-made forests – banana plantations, for example – which are within or close to their natural habitat. Here they can be very destructive, and there is some sympathy for crop-owners who kill or try to catch maurauding orangs in their gardens.

Later still orangs acquired a value as skins and skeletons for museums, and living specimens for zoos. During the mid-to-late nineteenth century when collectors were most active, the need to conserve stocks of orangs was hardly an issue. The Asian rain forest was still enormous, and the inroads made by collectors were tiny in proportion to existing numbers. But the scientific writings of the time make it clear that dead animals were on the whole considered more valuable and informative than live ones. The naturalist's skill in bringing down orangs from the trees with his rifle was often described in detail. How the animals lived – even what they looked like – were not. Alfred Wallace, the distinguished Victorian naturalist, wrote an account of his second meeting with orangs – then almost unknown to science or to the world outside south-east Asia – that is typical of the period.

About a fortnight afterwards I heard that [an orang] was

feeding in a tree in the swamp just below the house, and, taking my gun, was fortunate enough to find it in the same place. As soon as I approached, it tried to conceal itself among the foliage, but I got a shot at it, and the second barrel caused it to fall down almost dead, the two balls having entered the body. This was a male, about half-grown, being scarcely three feet high. On April 26th, I was out shooting with two Dyaks, when we found another about the same size. It fell at the first shot, but did not seem much hurt, and immediately climbed up the nearest tree, when I fired, and it again fell with a broken arm and a wound in the body. The two Dyaks now ran up to it, and each seized hold of a hand, telling me to cut a pole, and they would secure it. But although one arm was broken, and it was only a half-grown animal, it was too strong for these young savages, drawing them up towards its mouth notwithstanding all their efforts, so that they were again obliged to leave go, or they would have been seriously bitten. It now began climbing up the tree again; and, to avoid trouble, I shot it through the heart.

Practically all of Wallace's encounters with orangs ended with the death of one or more animals, and he was by no means unrepresentative of the naturalists of his time. Even the missionaries of the period seemed to regard orangs as creatures to be shot on sight. Of a mission settlement in Sarawak in 1865, the traveller Frederick Boyle wrote:

In especial the spot is haunted by *mias* (Malayan for orang utan), and, in fact, this is the only locality at present known where they can always be procured. The gentleman who we found assisting Mr Chambers in his mission labours has in the course of a few months shot eight of these animals, which are destructive, though in no way dangerous.

Tom Harrisson, the Malaya-based naturalist, from whose wife's book, *Orang Utan*, I took this quotation comments dryly in the introduction:

> Needless to say there have been no orangs anywhere near . . .
> within living memory. But when a single, unnamed, unre-
> corded padre could shoot eight in a few months . . . the
> amazing thing is that any orangs survived anywhere.

When zoos became fashionable, orangs were caught live and shipped out to Europe and America in enormous numbers. In 1878 William Hornaday, a famous American naturalist and collector, shipped at least forty out of Sarawak, and many other consignments must have left Malayan ports through the late nineteenth and early twentieth centuries. This trade has now fallen away considerably, thanks largely to better management within the zoos. This has ensured longer life for individual animals, and a higher proportion of new specimens being pro-vided by breeding in captivity. In 1965 the International Con-ference of Zoo Directors resolved to buy from the wild only animals that had been exported from Indonesia and Malaysia with legal export permits. In Indonesia the orang has been legally protected since 1934, and legal authority for export or ownership involves the personal signature of the country's president. However, orangs are still being bought and sold on the black market, as we were finding, and some are still being smuggled out of the country for sale to the less responsible zoos and to private collectors.

Within Indonesia a continuing threat comes from private collectors who are prepared to buy orangs despite their pro-tected status. The fashion began with wealthy Europeans of colonial days, whose gardens and houses were often decorated with cages full of local birds, reptiles and mammals. Today some of the more wealthy Indonesians keep up the tradition. Orangs and other primates were, and still are, favoured as pets. Caught as infants, they are kept several years until they grow big and uncertain of temper. Then they are handed over to zoos, destroyed or otherwise disposed of, to be replaced by another infant.

To capture a baby orang, the mother to which it is clinging is usually shot or clubbed to death. Frequently the baby plunges with her to its own death, or is so severely injured that it does not survive capture. Older infants are hunted down to separate them from their mothers, with whom they cannot keep up, and are snared or netted by the hunters. Many caught young die of under-nourishment, disease and infection, either in transit or in their captivity. It seems reasonable to reckon that, for every orang that reaches a private collection, at least three or four others die.

We were to see much of the effects of this trade during our years in Sumatra. Nearly all of the animals that came to our centre were taken from private ownership – sometimes amicably, sometimes under duress with the authority of the PPA weighing in. There were other sources of animals too. Orangs displaced when their forests were felled sometimes moved into plantations and gardens, creating a nuisance that required their removal. Occasionally we helped to capture orangs dispossessed when the trees were felled about them, transporting them for release elsewhere. But most of our animals – like Mania and the four who accompanied her to Mr Bangun's cage – were victims of the black market. The few we were able to recover in three years of work were only a proportion, though possibly a considerable proportion, of the total number in illegal captivity up and down Sumatra.

But Gersom's five were a welcome start. We resolved to find them proper accommodation and begin their rehabilitation as soon as possible.

4
Finding Bohorok

With the Rijksens back at their station in Ketambe I moved to
Kutacane, just a few miles down the Alas river, where the PPA
had a guest house. Now began a fretful period of waiting, with
very little I could do to advance our plans. From Kutacane I
reported back to Switzerland, sending estimates for the cost of
building the station and buying a Toyota. With no transport of
my own, I could only borrow the Rijksens' vehicle from time to
time, which restricted my efforts to find a site. The weather
didn't help. It seemed to be the hottest, stillest time of the year,
with heat brooding over the paddy fields day and night. Walks
were almost out of the question, and I was too far from the
forest to learn anything useful at first-hand about orangs. To
the local people I was the subject of unlimited, none-too-
friendly curiosity. I stayed indoors, read literature on primates,
took showers and drank tea to make up for the unnerving heat.
There was a short spell without rain. The water, which had to
be lifted in a bucket from a well, began to run out; the little that
was left took on an earthy, rotten smell that soon flavoured the
rice and tea. It was a dispiriting, unhappy time, with even
Markus away on another hunt for rhinos in the Gunung Leuser
Reserve.

But the gloom didn't last. The rains fell, the springs flowed
clear again, the air freshened, and our plans took an exciting
step forward. John MacKinnon, the biologist who had earlier

worked on the ecology of orangs in both Borneo and Sumatra, paid a brief visit to the Rijksens at this stage. I met him there, and talked over the problem of finding a station site. He drew my attention to the Langkat Reserve, the easternmost sector of the Gunung Leuser group of reserves. In particular he pointed me toward the area around the village of Bohorok, where he had spent a short time surveying wild orangs during his visit in 1971. This was not far from Medan, with a number of villages nearby. The reserve at this point had well-controlled boundaries, and there was known to be a wild orang population of reasonable density. Perhaps we should take Bohorok as a centre and work out from it?

From the map John and I picked on three possible sites that might make sense for our station. A good site would have to lie inside the Reserve, but not too far in and not too far from a road passable to vehicles. It must also be near a river, for two reasons. Firstly, a wide river would form a natural barrier to stop the orangs from wandering and possibly leaving the reserve, where their safety would lie both during and after rehabilitation. Secondly, a river would provide the unlimited supply of fresh water that would make everyday life in the tropical rain forest a great deal easier and pleasanter – my recent experiences at Kutacane had driven that lesson home. Finally, the site had to be reasonably close to civilization, and preferably not too far from a centre like Medan, so that we could buy our stores, enjoy a change of scenery and pace from time to time, and keep in touch with the people who would help us, both officially and unofficially, in our work with the apes. John's help and advice came at just the right moment, setting me on course once again.

So one day in April, after the rains had cleared the air, I borrowed the Rijksens' Toyota and set off with their driver, Pak Masirin. In Medan we picked up Mr Bangun, and headed for Bohorok, just over 2 hours drive away. Bohorok is a small village in the middle of extensive rubber plantations. Cleared

39

from the original forest, some of the plantations belong to British companies, and others are owned by the Indonesian state. Bohorok itself is a little more than a crossroads with thirty to forty houses, a police station, and three little cafés. The PPA had a small office and patrol base there – certainly a point in its favour.

Arriving in the midday heat, we started by reconnoitring the northernmost of the three areas I had marked out. This was the Sungei Kerapuh river, which ran, the map told us, between the plantations and the edge of the reserve. We climbed for more than an hour along the hillsides, mostly through young rubber plantations which did little to protect us from the intense heat. Eventually we reached a notice which said: 'Reserve starts here. Hunting and tree-felling forbidden.' There was no fence, and nothing else to protect the reserve at this point. The Sungei Kerapuh, our hoped-for boundary, turned out to be a narrow stream; by no stretch of the imagination could it be called a barrier for orangs suffering from wanderlust. Marching with the reserve, and separated from it only by this narrow waterway, the rubber plantations lay wide open. I could just imagine how the rehabilitated orangs would use the tops of the growing rubber trees as their gymnasium, tearing them to pieces and making themselves thoroughly unpopular throughout the district. The problems of keeping orangs out of the plantations – like the problem of keeping people out of the reserve – seemed insuperable at this point. Mr Bangun, who welcomed the prospect of having the reserve in his province, pointed out all the advantages, while I could see only the difficulties. So we returned to Bohorok for the night, arguing fitfully over the merits and drawbacks of Sungei Kerapuh.

There was no inn or guest house in Bohorok, so we decided to camp down for one night in the PPA's little two-roomed shack. In one room, furnished rather surprisingly with a large bed, slept Mr Bangun, Pak Masirin the driver, and two local PPA men who were helping us in our search. I was given the office. I pushed two desks together and unrolled my sleeping bag, and soon made myself comfortable; with even a well and a privy in the yard we were camping in comparative luxury. Just as I was about to doze off, Pak Masirin brought me two twisted incense sticks stuck into bottles. He lit the ends and they glowed, giving off aromatic smoke. *'Obat nyamuk,'* he remarked with a smile, 'mosquito medicine'. His medicine worked; not an insect disturbed me that night, though hordes could have entered the little office through cracks in the shutters and walls.

Next morning we headed for Sungei Landak, the Porcupine river, which was my second choice of site. This is a slow-running river, rather under 100 feet wide, lying in fairly flat lowlands. I had pinpointed on the map the place where the reserve boundary crossed the river, about $1\frac{1}{2}$ hours' walk upstream from the road. As there was no established path we walked in the river itself. This site appealed to me much more than the previous one, but the stream banks were narrow – too narrow for us to think of constructing a reliable road. And at the end of it, where river and boundary crossed, there was no ground flat enough for us to build our houses and cages. Despite its appeal, the Porcupine river site would never do.

Now I was almost at my wits' end. We had one more river to look at. What would I do if that too turned out to be unsuitable? With five orangs already waiting for me in Mr Bangun's garden, I faced the prospect of having to give up the whole project, throwing away four months' valuable experience because I couldn't find a site for the station. Though we were all weary, I couldn't wait another day for a decision; I insisted on going that same day to look at Sungei Bohorok, the next river along from the Porcupine river, where I had pin-pointed the third possible site.

Unlike the Porcupine river, the Bohorok is a clear, bubbling mountain river about 100 feet wide. Both banks rise almost vertically in a shallow gorge. The edge of the reserve runs down to the river only a few hundred yards from the road, and then follows the course of the river upstream. On the other side a narrow fisherman's track led along the water's edge. But the banks on either side were far too steep for us to negotiate and build on, and a walk up the stream showed that they continued steep for several miles. As we walked, my heart sank; each step took us further from the village and the road that would form our lifeline.

Then someone suggested we cross the river into the reserve and take a closer look at the other bank. We waded through its clear fast-flowing water, which came up to our hips and tried to push us over. Climbing up the opposite bank, I turned wearily to glance back to where the river disappeared round a bend, and suddenly saw it – the place we were looking for. It was the perfect site – about $2\frac{1}{2}$ acres of flat ground, with two thirds of its perimeter bounded by the river itself. Behind it the hillside rose steeply into dense forest. It would have been difficult to imagine a better spot. There was plenty of space for two houses and at least some of the cages. The river was within easy reach all round, and wide enough to act as a natural boundary which would help to keep the animals in the reserve, only a twenty-minute walk from Bukit Lawang, the nearest village and road-head. And it was a beautiful, serene place, where we could work happily and to good purpose. This time there was no argument; we drove back to Bohorok with light hearts and celebrated our find with a good meal and plenty of beer for the whole party.

Next day in Medan, Mr Bangun introduced me to a contractor whom he thought might be right for the job of building the huts and cages. I showed him my plans of the two houses and explained what I wanted, and he promised to draw up estimates. During the week that followed I waited impatiently for Markus to return from his travels. Though I was pretty sure the site was the right one, I valued his opinion and wanted him to look it over before finally committing myself – and the bulk of the project's funds – to the banks of the Bohorok.

Ten days later I stood again on the bank above the stream, this time with Markus. He was in no doubt that the site was good, and said so enthusiastically. Mr Bangun, who was again with us, forgot his customary reserve and let himself be infected by our enthusiasm. The three of us rushed about with tape measures, wooden pegs and hammers between the tall bamboos, looking for the best situations for the two houses. I was insistent that no trees should be felled, so we sited the houses between the existing tall trees and clusters of bamboo. The house for the staff we sited at the point where we had first set foot on the peninsula; it looked across the river to the fishermen's track, and the staff would be able to keep a lookout for visitors. Just next to it we planned the two quarantine cages, and our own house would stand about 200 yards further upstream, backed by wild banana trees and looking down over the wide river.

Then Markus and I scrambled up the steep slope behind the site to look for a place for the rehabilitation cages. These were the cages from which the orangs would finally be released to freedom, so we wanted them to stand within the wild forest. But I also wanted them far from the houses – at least 400 yards away and preferably more. This was so that the orangs, once liberated, would keep well away from the huts and the quarantine cages. At Ketambe cages and houses were closer together, and some of the liberated orangs seemed to find it difficult to break with the people and routines they had become used to. A few became importunate camp followers; instead of going back to the wild, as they were supposed to, they spent their whole time thinking up new tricks to stay with the humans and get hold of food. Sometimes they followed the keepers home and laid siege to them, even breaking in through the kitchen roof and helping themselves to whatever was going. Here at Bohorok I wanted to be sure that the orangs were well away from the houses, and would not associate houses, keepers and food together.

43

A little below the main ridge, well above the peninsula, was a flat piece of ground just right for the rehabilitation cages. Markus and I staked out sites for two cages, each about 20 feet by 7 feet. These would be big enough to be partitioned into two, and between them would hold all the animals we were likely to want to liberate at once. The forest grew thick around, so the animals would climb straight out of the cages and into the trees. Then we scrambled downhill to the main site, picked up Mr Bangun, and drove back to Medan in a state of wild excitement; we were raring to go.

What we really needed just then was a good fairy who would wave her wand and build the station overnight, so we could move in next morning and start work on the orangs. Instead we met the contractor, who knew nothing of fairies or wands, and whose only spell was one of unmitigated gloom. He had worked out his costing, and reached a figure far beyond our means. Like others with whom we dealt in Sumatra, he may well have felt that a European-based project on animal welfare, funded from one of the world's wealthiest countries, could not fail to be well endowed. We could only explain that we represented a charity, not a government organization, and that even world-wide charities run their projects on little more than shoestrings. Our contractor set his figure and stuck to it. Having worked before for the PPA, he felt himself in a strong position and was not prepared to budge an inch.

'I'll buy the wood in Medan', he said. 'Then there's the transport from Medan to Bukit Lawang – that will be pretty costly – and we'll have to hire carriers to hump the wood to the station – that won't be cheap either.'

'But where does the wood come from that you normally buy here?'

'From Bohorok.'

'So let's buy this wood in Bohorok. It'll be cheaper and the transport costs will be lower. . . .'

'No, I buy this wood in Medan. If you want to buy in

Banda Aceh

A C E H

Meulaboh

Blangkejeren

Pangkalan berandan

Kutatyan

Medan

Bohorok

INDIAN OCEAN

Kabanjaha

Pematangsiantar

Singkilbaru

SUMATRA

//// Reserve

The Reserve at Bohorok

Bohorok, I'm not having anything to do with it.' He was probably seeing his commissions on timber-purchase disappearing one by one.

'Well, maybe we can talk to another contractor?' I asked Mr Bangun. He shrugged his shoulders. 'I don't know any others', he said sadly.

Markus and I talked it over and decided to build without a contractor; we weren't sure how, but we could not pay this man his price, and that was that. Taking Sihombing, one of the PPA men, with us, we returned to Bohorok the following day and drove up and down the main street, looking for new buildings.

45

We saw some simple, pleasant-looking wooden houses, and asked one of the villagers who had built them. 'Pak Isa,' we were told, 'a builder from Bukit.' After asking around, Sibhombing led us to a café in a nearby hamlet, where we sat down and waited.

Apart from serving food and coffee, this was also the general store. Beside the long bench and table were shelves full of nails, string, sugar bags, cigarettes, chunks of green soap and boxes of matches, and open crates overflowing with cabbages, egg-plants, duck eggs, and coarse-cut pipe tobacco. From wires on the ceiling hung tin saucepans and water jugs, ladles, rubber sandals, and assorted nylon brushes. All this was contained in a space less than 10 feet square. The owner of the café and store was evidently the main businessman in the village, and the Mr Fix-it who organized everyone else. He brought us sweet black coffee in glasses standing on saucers. We drank it the Indonesian way, pouring a little coffee into the saucer and sipping it as it cooled. The fine coffee grounds stayed at the bottom of the glass. As we drank, the proprietor hovered nearby, sending out minions and receiving messages like a general in the field. 'Pak Isa will be here soon', he said.

Sure enough, Pak Isa suddenly appeared in the doorway. He was a shrivelled little man, looking older than his years, and he greeted us courteously. '*Solamat siang, Tuan* – good-day, sir,' he said to Markus, then stretched his hand out to each of us in turn. After each handshake he laid his hand on his chest with a little bow, signifying in the traditional way that his greeting came from the heart. We asked him to join us over coffee, and explained in broken Indonesian our plan for building houses and cages in the forest. Sihombing, who knew no English, at least knew what we wanted, and could polish up our stumbling phrases into presentable Indonesian. Pak Isa, a patient man, listened closely and with interest. He asked few questions, but seemed to be working it all out in his head as we went along. Then he quoted us a price – for transport, materials and work –

less than half the figure quoted by our contractor.

So the bargain was struck. Sihombing wrote out detailed specifications and contracts for Pak Isa, who would build the houses, for Pak Isa's cousin, who turned up just in time to secure the sub-contract for transporting everything to the site, and for the café owner who, in his role of Mr Fix-it, would procure wood, cement, nails, wire, and even the palm-leaf roofing. As a civil servant Sihombing lent an air of judicial respectability to the whole affair, and with earnest expressions the men set their signatures to the contracts – drawn up in Arabic script with many embellishing flourishes. They saw no reason why they should not start getting the materials together in the next few days, and promised that the smaller staff house would be ready by the middle of June.

Markus and I returned to Kutacane, more than happy to leave everything to our good fairy Pak Isa. That evening, relaxing in the guest house, Markus turned to me with a wink. 'Now we are going to build a home of our own', he said, 'we may as well do the thing properly and get married.' I smiled content-edly and nodded. To tell the truth, the same notion had occur-red to me more than once in the past few days; now I couldn't think of a better idea. 'Let's get married as soon as we can', I said. 'We'll go into Medan and see what we have to do about it.'

5
Settling In

'Getting married as soon as we can' took much longer than either of us expected. It was some weeks before we got to the registry office in Medan, and over three months before we were properly married under Indonesian law. Whatever the fashion in other parts of the world, marriage in Indonesia is a serious affair, not to be undertaken lightly on the spur of the moment. So we found when we faced the Medan registrar in the full majesty of his office.

'You can't possibly get married.' The registrar gazed at us severely over round spectacles, and picked his nose. We were standing in a long, narrow room, musty with heat and bureaucracy. The whole of one wall was covered from floor to ceiling with shelves of yellowing, dusty documents. A partition with shelves piled high stuck out 6 feet or more into the room. In between was a desk overflowing with papers.

'Why ever not?'

'No one can marry without their father's permission.'

'But we are both over twenty!' exclaimed Markus with astonishment.

'But you're less than thirty', countered the registrar. 'The law requires the father's written permission for anyone less than 30 years old.' 'And you have to obey the law too,' he added, in case we had missed the point.

We wrote off to our respective fathers in Switzerland for their permission in writing. Markus and I imagined them chuckling together as they exercised their parental powers – totally unexpected ones at that – for the last time. We fixed the wedding for early August, giving officialdom plenty of time to sort out matters in its own complex way. Markus returned to his rhinos, and I kept an eye on the situation at Bohorok, where building had already begun.

Meanwhile there was a new and welcome development – Regina arrived from Switzerland. She came by what seemed a long way round, via Rome, Tokyo and Singapore; it was an exhausted but very pleased Regina who met me eventually in a roadside café in Medan, one hot day in June. With her was Wumi, her little white Jack Russell terrier. Wumi sat wideawake under a chair and growled softly as I approached. However, she too was glad to see me once we had been introduced, and Wumi, Regina and I transferred quickly by bicycle taxi to a better café. Here we drank coffee and talked over everything that had happened in the past few months.

Regina and I scarcely knew each other. We had chatted a little about the orang project before I left Switzerland, and a number of letters had passed between us. Like me she had graduated in zoology at Zurich University, and served her apprenticeship orang management at Frankfurt Zoo. At that moment in Medan we really had no idea how our future work, and living together at close quarters in a tiny house, was likely to end – in friendship, incompatibility, or recrimination. We began that day in friendship, and I am happy to say that we stayed friends through all the problems, the failures and successes of the following years.

Regina arrived just as I was about to move into the first of the station buildings – the small house destined for later use by the staff. The day after her landing in Medan, we piled up the PPA Toyota with luggage, stores and station equipment and drove the 50 miles to Bukit Lawang. Here the road ended in front of a sugar-loaf of rock, completely overgrown with vegetation. Half covered by hanging fronds of fern, a cave-like passage ran past the sugar-loaf and through a minor maze of other rocks, finally opening onto a lush banana grove. The track was narrow and we had to walk in single file, with Wumi running happily in front.

Tropical rain forest is an odd setting for a small English Jack Russell terrier bitch to find herself, but Wumi, sophisticated by travel, took it all in her stride. Rome, Tokyo, Singapore, Jakarta – and now the rain forest; the world was full of interesting places for her to explore. She ran through the green shade of the banana trees, over a narrow bank between paddy fields in the full heat of the sun, and then into the jungle itself. She sniffed inquisitively into holes and dug her nose in the soft humus, relishing a whole host of new scents. She paddled and occasionally swam through the little streams that crossed the path. Now and again she looked back with a questioning glance: 'Am I going the right way?' When we made encouraging noises she trotted off again without hesitation. Behind us, the bearers carrying our luggage talked among themselves about the little white dog, fresh from overseas, who made herself so completely at home in the forest, and behaved as though she had lived there all her life.

After walking for 20 minutes we reached the banks of the Bohorok river, where the path came to an end. On the far side, across the boundary of the reserve, lay our new station. Now we had to wade the Bohorok. Wumi had already proved herself a strong swimmer in some of the small, fast-flowing streams, but here Regina carried her under her arm, just in case.

Crossing the Bohorok was always an adventure, varying with the level of water and strength of the current. With the river very low, the stones were covered with algal slime, so slippery that it was difficult to get a foothold. With rather more water the stones were much cleaner, but the current threatened to sweep your legs from under you. The local people seemed to find crossing easy enough, getting a really firm grip on the bottom with their strong feet and never losing their balance, even when the water was chest-high. Our feet, softened and weakened by shoes, were never quite up to it. On this first day our luggage and stores got across safely, but Regina and I fell over several times and Wumi got a bath too. We never minded a ducking; the water was never cold, but always chill and refreshing.

The staff house was already finished and ready to move in; our good fairy Pak Isa, well ahead of his schedule, welcomed us warmly to our new home and showed us around. Just behind the staff house was a durian tree, which the workmen were quick to point out to us. Durian, a famous – even notorious – south east Asian delicacy, is one of the Indonesians' favourite fruits. We were deemed especially fortunate to have a tree just by the house, where the fruits would practically fall into our lap. Already they were hanging, prickly as hedgehogs, from the branches above us; in a month or so they would be ripe and ready to fall. 'That's a particularly good kind of durian,' said Pak Isa with relish.

The little house had one bedroom and a roofed-in balcony. Like most of the local houses it was raised on stilts $2\frac{1}{2}$ feet above ground, allowing air to circulate freely underneath. Onto it at ground level was built a kitchen with an open hearth. Smoke from the fire escaped through slits in the back kitchen wall, and through the palm-thatched roof. We started by putting all our gear on the balcony and gradually sorting ourselves out. As well as suitcases we had brought up from Medan an assortment of mattresses, pillows, blankets, cooking utensils, Tilly lamps, kerosene lanterns, and a good supply of food. The two mattresses practically filled the bedroom. We knocked nails into the walls and stretched pieces of string to hang our clothes on. In the kitchen we stacked the tin plates, hung the cups on nails and put the rice and sugar into ant-proof containers.

Wumi made herself at home immediately and without fuss. She seemed to like the open plan of the house; it meant that she could make her rounds unimpeded from the river to the kitchen, to the bedroom, to the balcony, and out again to the nearby bamboos without annoying doors to get in her way, and without anyone shouting at her about dirty paw marks. After a first tour of inspection she lay down on one of our mattresses, curled up comfortably and took a rest from her long, busy day's work.

Meanwhile we had been out looking for firewood. It is not easy to make a fire in the rain forest; there is plenty of wood lying on the ground, but most of it is sopping wet and practically unburnable. Later we learnt to look along the river's edge for the wood of a particular kind of pine, highly resinous, that grows in the mountains and drifts down with the current. It burnt well in any circumstances; you could pick it out of the river and set fire to it straightaway. We found out where it collected and always kept a supply handy for kindling. But that was something we still had to learn; on that first evening we collected the driest bits we could find and tried to light them, coughing and swearing, with streaming eyes, in a smoke-filled kitchen. It took us an hour to get a little flame going, and another half hour to make our first pot of tea.

Then we went over to inspect the site of our future quarters. This was at the upstream end of the peninsula, with a bend in the river close by and surrounded by wild bananas, ferns and fronds of ginger as tall as a man. Wumi awoke and came with us. Refreshed after her nap, she sniffed importantly at the cement foundation piles, which were already in place. The workmen were making a frame of heavy joists which would fit over the piles, to carry the floor and walls. They used no machines, doing all their drilling, sawing and planing by hand. Beside the site was a primitive shelter with leaf-thatched roof, where the workmen slept. They would be here every day except Friday, Pak Isa explained; Friday was the day they returned to the village to pray in the mosque. We went back to the house. Our tiny fire had gone out. Before trying to light it again, we decided to go for a swim to get rid of the sweat and dust of the journey.

At the lower bend of the river the stream had carved a hollow at least 10 feet deep, making a perfect secluded swimming pool. The water, crystal clear and greeny-blue, swirled into shallows where the shingle glowed with orange and yellow dappling. We stripped off and jumped in; I have never known water so cool and refreshing as the Bohorok river, in our own pool, at the end of a hot day. We swam in circles within the pool and tried to make our way upstream against the strong current. Wumi stood barking on the bank until Regina eventually persuaded her to take the plunge. Then she too paddled happily in the bubbling water, emerging in the shallows to shake violently and plunging in again for another swim. Refreshed and clean, the three of us made our way back to the house, where we soon had the fire going again. By way of celebration we fried ourselves hamburgers, made on the spot from corned beef, eggs and crumbled cream crackers.

Night fell quickly at about half past six. With the darkness a full choir and orchestra of crickets and cicadas suddenly began to tune up all around us. We lit the lamps and made ourselves comfortable for the night. Moths, crickets and a dozen other kinds of insects swarmed in through the open windows to dance around the lamps. Wumi snapped at them and, rather to her surprise, caught a couple of moths. But she, like us, was sleepy and looking for a comfortable bed. We stretched out in sleeping bags on our comfortable mattresses; Wumi curled up in Regina's half-unpacked suit case. We blew out the lights and slept solidly, revelling in our first night at the new station.

Next morning we were awakened by Wumi's furious barking. We rubbed our eyes, slipped into our sarongs and looked out of the window. A little boy stood in front of the house, shouting '*Mawas, mawas* – orang utans', and gesticulating toward the village. This could mean only one thing – Mr Bangun had sent us the orangs which, for the last few weeks, had lived in the cage in his garden. We knew they had long outstayed their welcome, and that he was concerned about the health of one or two of them. We had looked forward to installing them in the quarantine cages – our first orangs, on their first step toward rehabilitation.

Locking Wumi safely in the house, we set off in high excitement for Bukit Lawang. There stood the green PPA Toyota with three boxes beside it in the grass. Naturally the news of the orangs' arrival had spread like wildfire in the village, and spectators crowded eagerly around. Some of the braver children were trying to peer through holes in the boxes, nudging each other excitedly and yelling with a mixture of enthusiasm and fear when something moved inside. They jumped back in real fear when the biggest box heaved and rocked, threatening to burst open at the seams. The PPA driver had a quick word with some of the local young men in Batak, a language we could not follow. They disappeared into the village, returning again in a few moments with wooden poles and ropes, which they quickly made into handles for carrying. In no time they had organized themselves into a carrying party, two to a box; lifting the poles onto their shoulders they swung off down the track to the station.

With the orangs had come our two helpers. Dekking Bangun, Mr Bangun's younger brother, was 22 years old. Thin and quiet, his long elegant fingernails suggested that he would have been better suited to an office job, had one been available on the station. But that was a first impression and a wrong one. During the next two years he became an enthusiastic and dedicated orang keeper; our work would have been sadly restricted in many ways without his willing, sensible help. The other man sent by the PPA to help us was in his late sixties. Though an experienced woodsman and fisherman, he found the work on the station too much for him and soon retired – to be replaced by another cousin of Dekking's.

We and our new station staff followed the bearers back to the quarantine cages, which fortunately the workmen had just completed. Both compartments were ready for occupation. Branches and bananas were already lying on the floorboards – an opening present from the workmen – and even the climbing bars were in place. We lifted the biggest box into one cage, shut the door behind it, and then opened the lid through the bars. It was an exciting moment. Though Gersom had sent us notes on each of the five orangs, and we had made their acquaintance some time before at Mr Bangun's, we had no idea which orang this particular case held, whether it was large or small, gentle or wild, calm or thoroughly ill-tempered after its uncomfortable journey. We had not long to wait. Hardly was the lock undone when the lid flew open and out stepped our first guest – Doli.

Doli in Batak means 'man', but this Doli was a girl. About 5 years old, she was strong and bumptious; her former owner had probably guessed her sex and named her from her tough, fearless character, without much regard for anatomical detail. Doli swung easily about her new cage, investigating the bananas and branches and staring quizzically at us one by one. Since the other boxes held two orangs each, we assumed that she was the largest, and gave her a compartment to herself for the time being. She seemed healthy, relaxed and quite self-possessed, and was soon munching the bananas happily on one of the shelves.

Out of the second box climbed Mania. She was the first orang we had met on the west coast, chained to the roof support of the forester's house. As such she had a special place in our affections. Since leaving the village she had filled out considerably on the good food Mr Bangun had provided. Her coat was still grey and her face serious, but her belly was fatter and her arms and legs looked far stronger than when we had first seen her. Mania took possession of her section of cage, and we watched with interest to see what else would emerge from the second box. Nothing happened, so Dekking and I tilted the box to see who was inside. We found a sad, red ball of fur cowering in the corner – a small female orang who clung tightly and had to be tipped out bodily. She was about the same age and size as Mania, but very different in temperament. The moment she slid out onto the floor of the cage, she rushed into a corner and turned her hairy back on us. We named her Singkil, after the port in the south of Aceh where Gersom had seized her from captivity. Clearly, Singkil was going to be a problem child, needing special care and attention.

In the third box were huddled two much tinier, sadder lumps of misery. Both were male and about 18 months old. One was called Rimba (meaning 'wilderness'). His head, shoulders and half his back were bare, and covered with an enormous scar. Rimba, we learnt, had emptied a pan of boiling water over his head in his former owner's kitchen. Though the wound had healed, Rimba had never recovered, remaining thin and dishevelled and thoroughly neurotic. The second little ape we named Cabe – Indonesian for red pepper. The colour was appropriate, but the rest of the name was an act of faith on our part. Sitting in the middle of the bananas, he clutched himself miserably with all four limbs, pouting and whimpering to himself. There was nothing in the least peppery about him, but we could only hope to restore some of his self-confidence and fire as time went on.

Regina and I stood in front of the cages and gazed at the five orangs with a mixture of excitement and concern. Wumi, whom we had let loose again, ran eagerly round the cages sniffing and wagging her tail. Doli stretched a long arm through the grille and seized her, gently but very firmly, by the scruff of the neck, lifting her and pulling her against the bars for a closer examination. Wumi had every right to panic and snap at her captor, but that was not her way of doing things. She seemed to regard the new arrivals as human rather than animal – perhaps more eccentric than most humans and smelling slightly different, but nevertheless to be treated with courtesy. She continued to wag her tail happily and Doli, satisfied with the inspection, put her down. From then on Wumi was perfectly content to be pulled about by the orangs, treating them rather as though they were children to be tolerated. The orangs were always intrigued by her and often played, but seldom hurt or ruffled her in any way.

The five orangs ate fruit and vegetables and drank milk copiously. Four of them seemed happy enough – even Rimba and Cabe cheered up after an hour or so and began to explore their cages. Only Singkil, the problem child, remained unhappy. She behaved stangely, seeming to fear not only us but her four companions as well, and refusing to do anything but huddle in her corner.

Whatever her problem, Singkil did not get over it. At the end of the first week, when the other four were settled, Singkil remained in her knot of misery, as unresponsive and fearful as she had always been. Then one morning Dekking came flying back from the cages with the news: '*Ada mawas mati* – an orang has died!' We hurried over, unbelieving, but Dekking was right; Singkil lay dead in the corner where she had huddled for the 8 days she had spent with us. We were completely at a loss; apart from her strange behaviour, she had shown no signs of physical illness, and had eaten and drunk like the others. But there was no knowing her sad history. She may well have been damaged – a head injury, perhaps – when she was originally captured or during her later confinement. It was a worrying, saddening business, making us doubly anxious about the remaining four.

Doli and Mania gave little cause for concern; there was always the chance that they too might succumb to a mysterious illness derived from their earlier treatment, though it seemed very unlikely. Rimba and Cabe continued to worry us; they were the weaklings, and didn't seem to be making the progress we expected. In our concern we took them back to the house in the evenings, so we could keep a closer eye on them. This was much against our general philosophy, which was to avoid at all costs making pets of the orangs; the last thing we wanted was to domesticate them. But these two needed special attention by night as well as by day, so they slept in one of the transport boxes under the shelter of our roof.

On the second night of this special treatment Rimba developed a high fever. It stayed with him through the morning and into the afternoon. We kept him all day in the house, in a box padded with clothes, giving him regular injections of anti-biotics. The fever went down after a few more hours, but had proved too much for the small, scarred body. His temperature continued to fall; by evening it was down to 35 °C and still falling, and by night-time it was no longer registering on our thermometer. We wrapped Rimba in blankets and filled an empty bottle with hot water to warm his bed. But during the night he fell into a coma, from which he never awakened. He died the next morning; weakness and undernourishment had given way to pneumonia, which finally killed him.

It would be hard to imagine a more depressing start to our work; with the apes on the station less than ten days we were already having to dig two graves. But these events strengthened our resolve to keep small or weak animals under special surveillance in the house right from the start, so that we could spot any illness sooner and deal with it more effectively. Neither Singkil nor Rimba died entirely in vain. Both taught us lessons which we put to good use later in our dealings with other orangs.

Before the end of the second week we were cheered by the return of Markus from one of his rhino expeditions. Regina scarcely knew him; for Wumi too he was a stranger, to be greeted with the appropriate fury of barking. But Markus charmed Wumi by playing with her, tickling her behind the ears; he soon won her undying friendship. Regina too came to appreciate him – though not for the same reason! Markus and she got on well from the start. He often returned from his fieldwork just when we most needed counsel and support. He never tried to organize us or run the station his way, but his masculine point of view and his practical help were always appreciated. The three of us formed a strong team, complementing each other in all kinds of useful ways.

Six weeks after our first application for marriage, Markus and I presented ourselves again before the registrar. Permission to marry had been granted, in writing, by our respective fathers, and we saw no reason for further delay. But we had underestimated the registrar. He remained unmoved.

'You can't get married.' This time he didn't even look at us, but rummaged importantly in files that had remained undisturbed for years.

'Why not? We've brought you our fathers' permission; what's wrong now?'

'Your fathers have written their permission in German, and I can't understand it.'

We explained to him that, for their part, our fathers didn't understand Indonesian, but that wasn't going to stop us getting married. The registrar conceded the point, but was not in the least dismayed. A short pause for thought, and his face lit up again.

'But you still can't get married. You see, we don't know whether your superior approves.'

That was a fairly easy one to cope with. We didn't waste time arguing, but came back next morning with Mr Bangun. Though we were originally put into the field by Frankfurt Zoo, technically the PPA was our employer in Indonesia, and Mr Bangun was their senior representative. As a civil servant, and probably more senior than the registrar, Mr Bangun carried some weight. He solemnly gave his assent to our marriage, and we waited with baited breath for the registrar's next move.

He had no more to say just then, keeping his final shot for 30 July, two days before the date fixed for the wedding. We drove again into Medan to make sure all was well.

'You can't get married.' There was no mistaking the triumph in his voice. 'The bans must be published three weeks in advance, to see whether anyone has any objections to the marriage.'

'But not a soul here knows us. Who could object? Anyway, you've got the papers from our home villages that say we can be married.'

'It's what the regulations say. You can't go against the regulations.'

'Why didn't you tell us this a month ago? Then there'd have been plenty of time. We've asked all our friends for the day after tomorrow.'

'So you don't want to obey the regulations like everyone else?'

'Do you think we could talk to your boss about this?'

The registrar pondered, muttering irritably.

'Come back tomorrow', he said finally.

The following morning we stood before him again. We had decided to put off the legal ceremony for three weeks if necessary, but to have the party and the honeymoon, which were already laid on, just as we had planned.

'The head registrar says it might be possible to make an exception. That of course means . . . special arrangements.'

'We understand that. But of course we are very grateful to you for being so very helpful. . . .'

'Only if someone now raises and proves an objection, you'll have to take the consequences.'

We both signed a form accepting full responsibility, should there prove to be anything illegal about the wedding. Then we signed a second form, the promise of marriage: 'Markus B. and Monica L. promise each other their hands in marriage. Since no-one has raised any objection to this marriage over a period of three weeks, this promise of marriage is valid under law.' As simple as that . . .!

On 1 August we were back at the registry office, dressed up to the nines. Regina and a Chinese friend were to be witnesses. There was another couple in front of us – a sweet young bride in pink lace, who modestly murmured the necessary "Yes". Surrounded by fragrant mothers and grandmothers adorned with flowers, and fathers with serious expressions, bride and bridegroom left the registry office in an aura of radiance.

Then it was our turn. Regina was the most excited of us all. She had never been witness at a wedding before, and was sure we weren't taking the whole thing seriously enough. The registrar smiled benevolently, as though he personally had been responsible for smoothing our path to marriage. Then he coughed and read out our future duties to us.

'First, although you are now married, you must continue to love and respect your parents.'

'Second, man and wife must live together under the same roof.' (That would be difficult in our case; with me watching orangs and Markus chasing rhinos, we'd be lucky to see each other once every month or two.)

'Third, the husband must love the wife and the wife must obey the husband.'

So it went on for all of 5 minutes. At the end of this address the registrar smiled knowingly and said: 'There's so much talk of family planning today that we think it right to advise young couples not to have too many children. You really shouldn't have more than five or six these days.'

We nodded agreement and signed our marriage lines.

We'd made it – we were man and wife at last. In front of the registry office were hordes of *becas* – bicycle taxis. We chose two of them for our wedding coaches. Markus and I travelled in the first, and the two witnesses followed. So we processed across Medan to our wedding party, and Markus and I to a brief honeymoon well away from orangs, rhinoceroses and overzealous registrars.

6
In Business at Last

On our return from honeymoon we set about moving ourselves
and our belongings into the larger house. Pak Isa and his men
had not yet finished. The cages were still to be completed and so
was the promised furniture – beds, tables, chairs and shelves;
but there was enough to be going on with. We made ourselves at
home again on the floor. This pleased Wumi; it was easier for
her to stick her nose into everything. We had a bathroom, but
so far no water. The day we returned, Markus started to lay on
water to the house from a nearby stream, using 300 yards of
plastic hose. Below the station the stream plunged down a
frothing waterfall into the Bohorok, but the gradient between it
and our house was just enough to provide us with constant
running water. Now we could wash up in the kitchen, instead of
having to carry everything down to the river, and wash or bathe
with plenty of water whenever we felt like it.

'Your Bohorok river is going to be a problem', said Markus
over supper. 'The big rains may start in October, and when its
constantly in spate you could be cut off from the village for days
at a time. You two can probably swim over, but how will you get
food and orangs across?'

I'd thought of this too. 'I've been asking around where we
might buy a canoe', I said. 'They aren't used very much in these
parts because the rivers are small and people can generally cross
on foot.' That meant that no-one knew how to build them

locally. The nearest place we could buy one was Besitang, north of Medan. But just at that time the rice harvest was keeping all the farmers busy in the paddy fields, and no one had time or inclination to build a boat. 'I don't think we'll get a dugout before February,' I said, 'and by then the heaviest rains will be over.'

'Well, what about a cable railway', said Markus. 'Then at least we'd get food and baggage across.' This was Markus at his most practical. I saw he was itching to start work on one straight away. So we ordered a *perahu* in Besitang, and bought wire rope, grips, pully-blocks and all the trimmings for a cable railway to tide us over. Markus and the men set to work, and soon we had a railway in operation. Everything we wanted to take across the river was put into a big shopping basket, which hung from a hook and could be pulled to and fro. At about this time we heard that the Frankfurt Zoological Society would be sending us a Toyota in the spring. This was good news indeed; it was the one important item we needed to make the station fully operational.

We lived simply, cooking in our tiny kitchen which also served as a laboratory. Our staple food was rice, livened up with tinned mackerel and sardines, peanuts and cream-cracker biscuits. From a nearby village we could buy duck eggs and sometimes a tough chicken. Vegetables were plentiful, but the choice was usually limited to egg plant, cabbage, bananas and cucumber. With their wide range of spices the Indonesians charm delicious dishes out of these unexciting raw materials, but our efforts to ring the changes often led to very strange mixtures indeed. I still remember a vegetable casserole of egg plant, bananas and peanuts, which we threw together in a hurry and never repeated.

When we grew tired of the monotonous diet of village food, we could shop further afield in Bohorok or Medan. Mr Bangun often sent us his Toyota on Sunday, which was market day in Bohorok, to help with the shopping. The large and abundant market at Medan furnished us with flour for baking our own bread, fresh meat for stews and curries, and a variety of vegetables and fruit. These luxuries were perishable and had to be eaten up quickly. We lived well for a few days after each visit to market, then the menus gradually deteriorated until we were back on cabbage and rice. After two or three weeks we were glad of another opportunity to buy fresh supplies and cook ourselves more good food.

Bohorok too had a lively, colourful market to which the peasant women came from far around with their produce. Long before we got to the village we would be overtaking country women with heavy bundles on their heads, and men pushing bicycles piled high with produce. The better-equipped came in carts drawn by oxen or water-buffalo. The market stalls were filled with food, and there was a wide choice of other Indonesian local produce – tempting sarongs and Batik cloths, woven mats and basket-work objects of every shape and size. It was fun to rummage and bargain for goods, though better for our finances if we stayed away. We didn't go there solely for the fun of it. Here in the market we met the local people and picked up gossip; we could sense different attitudes to our conservation work, and occasionally gather useful information about captive orangs.

Back at the station we enjoyed watching the builders as they put the finishing touches to everything. Pak Isa, the *tukang rumah* or master builder, managed everything with quiet confidence and efficiency. His carpenters and thatchers got on with their jobs, knowing what to do and working with the simplest of tools, some of which they had obviously made themselves. Our detailed plans, that I had worked so hard over, were treated as guidelines rather than instructions; Pak Isa and his men knew how to build houses, working by discussion and inspiration rather than formal plans. They built the houses the wrong way round and altered some of the proportions, but we didn't mind;

they worked steadily and willingly, and made a good practical job of everything. Now the living quarters and quarantine cages were completed, they had only the rehabilitation cages to build up on the hillside.

Every few days we climbed up into the forest to see how they were getting on. Built of heavy timber, with thick iron bars, these cages seemed almost too strong for their job. But orangs too are very strong, as I had seen at the Rijksen's, and they are much more persistent than most other apes. They have been known to use branches and planks as levers to break their way out of confinement, and to work away at any weakness quietly and persistently until they get what they want. So we used the best materials Pak Isa could lay hands on, and we built strong. The climb up to the cages was steep, and helped to keep us in good condition.

At first our only visitors from the outside world were fishermen, who often passed close to the station when they were working the river. We exchanged greetings with them, and watched them when we could. Their wiry bodies seemed fully at home in the water; I never saw one slip or fall on the treacherous cobble-stones. They were past masters at casting their special nets – *jalas*. Markus learned the trick of throwing them, but we never managed it; the nets are much heavier than they look, and take a lot of handling skill. The equipment the fishermen carried varied with how long they intended to stay out fishing. For a day trip a *jala* and a *parang* (jungle knife) were all they needed. But if they were going upstream to Simpang Dua, when two streams combine to form the Bohorok, they took rattan baskets full of rice, coffee, chillies, sugar and tea, to sustain them on their journey.

We sometimes bought their fish, which were mostly small and very bony; they were a pleasant change from our tinned fish. But when the fishermen caught an *ikan dong-dong* – a big eel-like fish with juicy, tender flesh, weighing up to 10 pounds – they could always rely on us as customers. Markus had learnt how to cook them on one of his expeditions in the forest, cutting them into strips and smoking them, preferably overnight, on a small fire. Unfortunately this was a rare treat; *ikan dong-dongs* (we relished the name almost as much as the fish) were difficult to catch, and something of an event. The fishermen had to use special rods and lines, and drop their hooks (baited, of course, with highly special and secret bait) into deep clefts in the stream bed – only there were *ikan dong-dongs* found.

There were wild fruits in plenty, though not many that we could enjoy. However, we feasted when our own durian tree began to drop its ripe fruit. Prompted by the builders, who had earlier pointed out their virtues, we explored one of the football-sized fruits rather tentatively. We pushed our fingers into the cracks (' . . . just like orangs', said somebody very aptly) and ripped the rough, thorny skin apart. Inside the fruit was divided into five segments, with 4 or 5 stones the size of a plum in each. The stones lay buried in a pale orange, cheese-like pulp, which looked unappetizing and smelt strongly of rotting onions. Clawing the stones out of the husk, we tasted the flesh very cautiously. It was a strange flavour, like nothing we had ever tasted before. It took several weeks and a lot of experimenting before we realized why everyone made a fuss about durians, and became durian addicts ourselves.

Wumi was less impressed. She examined a half-chewed stone, sniffed it, sneezed, and left it alone. Our three orangs took a more favourable view, sucking dreamily at the stones like children with ice-cream, eyes half-closed in bliss. Once out of their quarantine cages and free to wander, they found the durian tree and spent a lot of their time there. The workmen too had their share. Our durian tree was all that they had promised.

In September Mania, Cabe and Doli finished their quarantine period and graduated to the newly-completed rehabilitation cages. Here they were more remote from contact with people, and could spend a few weeks in relative peace and quiet, getting used to the sounds and sights of the green wilderness

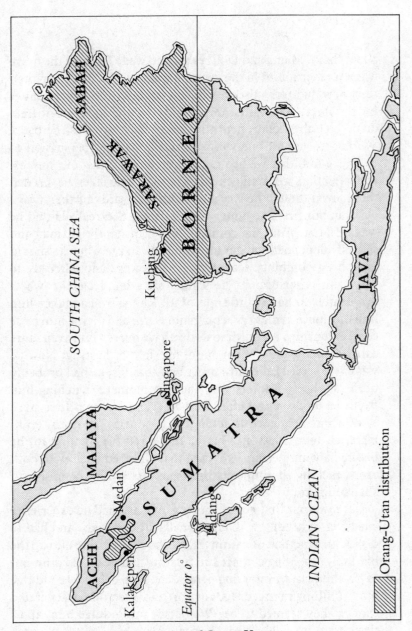

Distribution of Orang Utans

about them. Mania and Doli responded well. To them the move was a further round in the exciting game of life. They explored their new quarters, discovered new interests and opportunities for mischief, and waited impatiently for the moment of freedom. To Cabe – poor, neurotic Cabe – the move was a setback. We had to use all our patience and powers of persuasion to convince him that we had not deserted him – that our interest and affection were still at his disposal whenever he needed them, even though he was a few hundred yards further away.

From our first encounter with Cabe we had realized that he was different from his companions – constantly anxious and pitifully dependent on our attention. At an age when he should have been climbing, scampering, exploring, and all ready to play with other orangs, he simply sat around on his own, a desperately unhappy little ape. With Rimba we had taken him into the house at night, keeping him warm and giving him close companionship. After Rimba's death we nursed him even more carefully and were seldom out of his sight or hearing. Now he was alone again. Like most other baby orangs, he had probably been caught by hunters who shot his mother, snatching him from her body long before he had taken his own first steps toward independence. Lacking body contact, warmth, milk, maternal tenderness and his mother's red fur to cling to, he became a whimpering little mite that clutched itself with both arms, rocking rhythmically back and forward in the misery of abandonment.

Cabe was our first neurotic orang. We had had no experience whatever of dealing with emotionally sick animals, and had to decide on a method of treating him. Should we bring him up the hard way, avoiding contact and trusting that he would grow out of his childish, whimpering dependence? Or should we indulge him, fulfilling his needs for comfort and affection, exaggerated though they seemed to be? We decided to indulge him, and I think we were right. We let him sit on our laps, clutch us, suck at our ears and fingers, and express all his need for physical contact with our warmth. There was a deal of pent-up emotion involved. If we tore ourselves away from him to get on with our other work, he cried desperately and immediately began hugging himself, rooted to whatever spot he happened to be standing in. Cabe was a tribulation, who drew out of us every reserve of patience – far more than either of us had dreamed we possessed.

We began our therapy during his quarantine period, and now continued it at the rehabilitation cages. Each time we climbed the hill we made a point of handling Cabe, holding him tightly and letting him play with us. He stroked and hugged us, often falling asleep on our laps. Sometimes we gave him his daily ration of milk from the bottle, when he would cling to us and drink like a little baby. Gradually we noticed a change in him. Still hungry for love and attention, he grew calmer, accepting our evening departures philosophically. As time went on he became much more independent, drawing a little away from us during our visits, climbing near to us and eating leaves, though never out of sight or easy reach. Soon he was spending whole days on his own, exploring cautiously in the forest close at hand, and slowly picking up the techniques of climbing that he had never had the chance to learn with his mother.

In the late afternoons and evenings, when we approached for our daily visits, Cabe would climb toward us carefully and deliberately, like a child demonstrating a new skill. Sometimes he whimpered with frustration and annoyance at his own clumsiness, especially if we moved away faster than he could follow. When these close daily contacts were interupted for a few days by our absence, Cabe suffered a relapse. Coming back after a break, we would find him anxious and neurotic again, clutching us tightly as before and crying when we locked him into his cage at night. But extra attention soon put him back on the right track, and over the months his improvement was beyond doubt.

Cabe took all of 3 years to overcome his impediment of

arrested development. As I write now, he is over 5 years old and has at last caught up with himself, developing into what seems to be a perfectly normal, half-grown orang. His behaviour matches that of other 5-year-olds. He builds nests and sleeps in them at night, finds his own food, and even plays cheerfully with other orangs. No longer dependent on human contact, he withdraws if people come too close and spends most of his time in the forest. Soon he will have reached complete independence, and be ready to leave the station altogether.

We visited the three orangs several times daily while they were in the rehabilitation cage, and Dekking and the other staff kept an eye on them too. We took food at mid-afternoon, and gave them green, leafy branches each evening so that they could practise building nests. This was not just a form of occupational therapy, like weaving and basket-making in a hospital ward. The urge to build came upon them each evening for a few minutes before they settled to sleep. It was a pattern of behaviour essential to them in the forest, where the nest or sleeping platform, built anew each night, kept them safe in the tree-tops and well away from ground predators. By giving them materials we encouraged them to develop the nest-building habit. After some days in the cages, we opened the doors and let them roam. They always stayed close at hand, delighted to be free at last but never wandering far and usually returning without prompting to their cages at night.

Releasing the orangs for the first time proved quite an adventure, especially for Wumi. She had to be present, of course, when we opened the cage door for Doli, Mania and Cabe, and she watched with interest as the three took their first tentative steps toward freedom. Doli and Mania, the two young females, did what most healthy orangs do in the circumstances; they climbed the nearest tree. Cabe, less enthusiastic, had to think things over and worry about them for a while. Wumi leapt up at the tree, yelping excitedly to see her playmates disappearing so fast. After a few minutes Doli came down a little and hung by her feet from one of the lower branches, so that her hands almost touched the ground. Wumi ran up to her and Doli, head downward, gave her a friendly tickle. Wumi began to snap playfully at Doli's face. Doli dropped to the ground, made a grab at Wumi, got a firm grip of her, and draped the little dog round her neck like a duchess with a silver fox fur. Holding Wumi's four legs in front with one hand, she climbed back up the tree.

By the time we had seen what was happening it was too late to interfere; Doli was already 10 feet up. Wumi seemed bewildered but quite at ease, lying calm and relaxed about Doli's neck. There was nothing we could do; calling and enticing with bananas had no effect – Doli swung idly, climbing a little with her free hand and feet and still holding firmly onto Wumi. Then, about 15 feet above the ground, she tired of the game. Picking off Wumi by the scruff of the neck, she held her out at arm's length and let go. Whimpering, and now thoroughly frightened, Wumi dropped like a stone. Luckily she made a soft landing on a fern bush and wasn't hurt. But from that moment onward she took more care in her dealings with the orangs. She played only with the very small ones, and particularly avoided Doli. One rough game was enough with these strange, unpredictable four-handed children.

Shortly after the first three moved up the hill to the rehabilitation cages, three more young orangs arrived from the west coast. Gersom, the energetic PPA representative in Aceh, had seized them from illicit captivity after only a few weeks in cages, so they were still fairly wild and in good health. Gamat, a female of 2 years or so, and Bako, a young male, were put together in one quarantine cage. Lela, an older female of about $4\frac{1}{2}$, had a compartment to herslf. So now we had six orangs, all young, well developed and healthy, comfortably settled in their various cages and progressing satisfactorily toward release. Thinking back only a few weeks, to the dark days when Singkil and Rimba died, we seemed to have come a long way, and learnt a lot about our job from the orangs themselves.

7
Expeditions are Hell!

Markus was back and ready to leave again, this time for an expedition into the wild country between Bohorok and Kutacane to the west of the Langkat Reserve. Markus wanted to scout around for rhinoceros spoor, and I was keen to examine areas some distance away from the station where we might be able to release orangs. So I joined his party. No one had crossed the Reserve this way before, but it seemed a straightforward proposition – up to the headwater of the Bohorok river, and over a col to the source of another stream – the Lawe Kingo – which would lead us down into the Alas valley. 'Six days altogether,' said Markus cheerfully, 'and we'll carry a couple of days' extra rice in reserve.'

It was unsurveyed country. We studied the best map we could find, but didn't altogether trust it. We hired several bearers to carry the camping equipment and food, and Mr Bangun, our friend from the PPA, decided to come too. And we also took Pawang Husin, a guide whom Markus had come to know and trust during his months of travelling in northern Sumatra.

Pawang Husin is a quiet, wise man of about sixty. In the old days he used to hunt rhinoceroses and sell their horns, skin, teeth and bones as medicine. Because he knew the forest so well, the PPA had taken him on as a game warden, and it was in this capacity that Markus had asked him to accompany him as a guide on his first expedition, several months earlier, to the rhinoceros areas of the Gunung Leuser Reserve. A deep friendship quickly grew between them, and Pawang Husin went with Markus on every one of his expeditions during the next three years.

Although the Pawang had previously hunted rhinoceroses, he understood perfectly why they now had to be protected. 'All creatures have the right to live on our earth. If all the rhinoceroses got killed, even God could not give them back to us.'

'Pawang' is an honoured title in Aceh, granted to men who stand in a special relationship to nature and her spirits or soul and know many mysterious secrets of the forest. To make sure he doesn't lose the knack of communicating with the spirits of the forest, a Pawang must always do his best to behave honourably and fairly to his fellow men. Naturally enough this enhances the regard in which the community holds him. Pawang Husin is a Muslim but an animist too. 'How can you say the river has no soul? See how it flows, bubbles over stones and foams through gorges? Could it do that if it wasn't alive?'

The logic of his arguments often left Markus's knowledge of physics standing. One evening the bearers were discussing what caused the tide to ebb and flow. Markus held forth with long-winded explanations about the phases of the moon and forces of attraction. The Pawang listened politely, then smiled and said quietly: 'It's much simpler than that. You all know the little crabs that live in holes on the beach. When they're all sitting in their holes it's flood tide. When they all come out the water flows into the holes and then it's the ebb.'

They all laughed in sympathy with Markus, because he'd given them such a complicated explanation when it was really all so simple. It was quite true – you only saw the little crabs outside their holes at ebb tide.

Pawang Husin is not a magician, in whose powers you have to believe superstitiously. His wisdom is based on a great gift of observation and a deep feeling for nature; it was this that brought Markus more and more under his spell. Many of his principles could be explained in terms of Western modes of thought. 'In the forest you mustn't carry any weapon except a jungle knife. If you come unarmed, the spirit of the mountain knows you have no evil intentions and have just come to look. He will make sure nothing happens to you.' This was one of the first precepts he gave Markus, and it made good sense in Western terms. Carry a gun, and you may well be tempted to behave impetuously in a critical or dangerous situation. Unarmed, you're hardly likely to try and show off to a tiger or an elephant, and they are less likely to be roused to attack.

Pawang Husin often sat at night beside the fire, gazing into the darkness and listening. Sometimes he spoke softly and urgently to the air, and Markus learnt that he was adjuring 'Harimau' the tiger to steer clear of the open camp with its sleeping men. When Markus asked how the Pawang knew a tiger was around, he simply said: 'I felt it.' Every time this happened, Markus found a tiger's fresh footprints close to the camp on the following morning.

The Pawang's special gifts came sharply into focus one day in the forest a few months later. For over a year Markus had been following rhinoceros spoor. He'd spent weeks crouching high up in a hide between two rhinoceros runs and had followed fresh tracks for several days. But not once had he seen one of these shy animals. On this particular morning the Pawang suddenly said: 'Today you'll see a rhinoceros.' Markus raised his eyebrows in disbelief; Pawang Husin had never made a prophecy like this before. They kept on the move the whole day, finding a fresh rhinoceros track and following it until evening drew in. But they couldn't catch the animal up. The Pawang's words had not been fulfilled and Markus was a bit disappointed as they went back to camp together.

Then, as they were sitting at supper, a low-slung dark colossus suddenly burst out of the undergrowth, thundered puffing and snorting past the camp and disappeared into the bush again. The spoor it left behind showed the animal had been eating leaves quite near the camp. He had probably first spotted the green plastic roof and smelt the fire and men when he was right on top of them. He took to his heels in fright, right past the astonished men. It was the only time Pawang had prophesied a rhinoceros. It never happened again – and that was the only rhinoceros Markus saw face to face in three years.

Four days out on the excursion to Kutacane, our expedition was stuck on the steep side of a mountain, in the network of ridges and valleys that form the western boundary of the Langkat Reserve. There was no level ground to pitch camp. We crouched exhausted on the mountainside with no supper in prospect, because we hadn't found any water nearby either. We would be counting on over-night rain for our early morning tea. Markus told the bearers to stretch plastic sheets on the ground and over our heads, so that we should at least be protected from the wet above and below. I took off my shoes and socks and crept into my sleeping bag. I managed to find a hole in the ground for my hips, but had to twist the upper part of my body to keep my shoulders clear of roots. I shoved my feet against some other roots to stop me slipping down the slope. Markus had contorted himself into an equally uncomfortable sleeping position, and Mr Bangun, Pawang Husin and the bearers were no better off. We lay in the dark, twisted and uncomfortable on the cold forest floor, longing for the morning when we could get up and leave that dreary campsite. Astonishingly, I must have dropped off to sleep, for I awoke to the sound of rain drumming on the plastic roof. By the light of a flickering hurricane lamp, two bearers were collecting water in a saucepan from a gutter they had made in the plastic. Contentedly I fell asleep again – soon there'd be a wonderful cup of tea.

It was the Pawang who woke me in the morning. He was holding in his hands a plate piled to the brim with dry rice and dried fish. *'Makan duluh* – something to eat first', he said courteously. I was very thirsty, and none too patient. 'I'd rather have a drink first. Isn't there any tea?' 'No, there was only enough water to wash and cook the rice.'

It wasn't what we wanted at all. Markus and I would much rather have just quenched our thirst and gone hungry, but obviously with the Indonesians it was the other way round. We said 'No' rather grumpily to breakfast, stretched our aching limbs and began to pack. One of Markus's shoes had been sticking out from under the roof and was half-full of water; he made a face as he pulled it on. When we were all ready to move, we started to climb straight up the side of the mountain, retracing our steps of the evening before.

Our suspicions of the map were well founded. After four days of following the Bohorok to its source, we should – according to its guidance – have crossed the watershed and found the Lawe Kingo without difficulty. Having reached the watershed on the fourth day, according to plan, we discovered something the map did not tell us; it was impossible to climb down into the valley. The river lay in a deep gorge between mountain-sides that were almost sheer. We couldn't find any animal tracks, which usually show the best way across country. The slopes were covered with prickly bracken thickets, so thick that we couldn't tell where the slope was passable: the ground was completely hidden. We had somehow to try and break through to the river, which would give us the direction out of the mountains into the inhabited Alas valley.

Two of our party hacked a narrow tunnel through the thicket with their parangs and we followed in single file. Now and then the bearers, who were all barefoot, stopped and used their parangs to gouge rattan thorns out of the hardened soles of their feet. So progress was slow. Towards evening we really thought we should soon reach the river. What we reached instead was the brink of a rock wall, with a sheer drop of 1,000 feet to the river below. So with the distant torrent roaring sardonically in our ears we spent yet another uncomfortable night on an incline. Next morning we climbed back up it, intending to contour westwards and find another place to get down to the river. Even here the going was extremely difficult. The bearers took it in turns to hack the path out, for there was still no sign of animal tracks. We climbed, slipped, sweated and scratched our hands to pieces. That evening we had still not found a way down to the river, and had barely made a mile of progress after 10 hours of very hard work. Yet another night on a slope dampened our enthusiasm considerably; but at least this time we found a stream, and enjoyed a lavish evening meal of rice and hot sweet coffee.

On the afternoon of the seventh day we at last got to the river. Happily we strode downhill along its bank without having to cut our way. But our luck didn't hold for long: after a few miles the river entered a steep-sided gorge and cascaded over a precipitous 35 foot waterfall. There was no path alongside it, and no way round it that anyone could see, without a long scramble up and across the slope, away from the water.

But then one of the bearers spotted a way of getting over the obstacle. There was a fallen tree lying diagonally across the cascade, with the remnants of its crown resting on the rocky bank below. Without hesitation or waiting for argument he clambered down the slippery trunk to show how easy it was. Having got to the inverted fork of the tree, he made 4 or 5 feet hand over hand along a branch, with his legs dangling. Reaching the rock wall, he quickly found a toehold. Now pressed hard against the rock, he nimbly climbed down the remaining 10 feet to the flat bank on the other side, throwing his arms in the air like a triumphant footballer and cheerfully waving us on.

The remaining bearers began to climb down with their packs on their backs. For me it was too much of an assault course; I didn't much care for it, and Mr Bangun wasn't looking any too happy either. But Markus and Pawang stood by to help and I hesitantly set foot on the wet, downward-sloping trunk. Pawang Husin went in front of me as I glissaded down on my bottom – at least that way I wouldn't lose my balance. My legs were soaked with fine spray. That I made it to the rock wall was a testament to my fear of falling, and to the Pawang's steadying hands. Pressed against the rock beside me, he showed me one by one which crevices and bumps to use as hand-holds as we climbed down. I still didn't like it, but his help made all the difference. Soon we were all down, and striding once again along an easy downhill stream bank.

That evening we found a flat site, and for a change made a comfortable camp. Markus and I were now getting worried because the stocks of rice were gradually running out, and we were still deep in the forest with 2 to 3 days' march ahead. On the following day, the expedition's eighth, we had to leave the river again because it ran through a gorge. Once again we scrambled up the steep overgrown slope and struggled westward with the stream sounding below. At midday we ate our last rice ration – quite a substantial meal, but 2 hours later the bearers laid down their loads.

'We can't go any further', they said.

'You'll have to', said Markus. 'It's still quite a way to Kutacane and anyway – you can't just sit here', he added pragmatically.

'There's no more rice and we have no strength left', they said in desperation.

'But it was only a couple of hours ago you stuffed your bellies full! You haven't had time to be hungry yet. And the faster we get off, the sooner you will get to Kutacane and have a good meal.'

'We have no strength left.'

There was no more to say. Silently Pawang Husin, Mr Bangun and Markus shouldered their packs, and I followed them doggedly. As I, a mere woman, was showing no outward signs of weakness, the bearers had no alternative but to save face and follow. Towards evening we got down to the river again and pitched camp. This time Markus and I were more than happy with our tea, but the poor bearers insisted they would die of hunger on the spot. It wasn't a happy situation. But we had no rice left, and there was nothing we could do but press on to Kutacane as quickly as possible.

The following morning we came to another waterfall and our spirits wilted. Pawang Husin scrambled up an overhanging bank and disappeared into the bush. 'This way,' he called down as he reappeared after a few moments, 'I've found a *rentis*.' This was a trace of a path hacked with parangs, and a sure sign of civilization. Now it really couldn't be far to Kutacane. I roped up, and with new-found eagerness two bearers pulled me up the bank, so fast that my head whirled. Markus and the Pawang were already probing the track ahead. We had no worries about following it; downhill, it could only lead to the Alas valley. Around noon we saw Kutacane lying at our feet, and four hours later we were in the village.

Soon we were all sitting happily in the inn, sipping tea with our tired legs stretched out in front of us. Inquisitive villagers crowded round.

'That was one hell of an expedition', said Mr Bangun. In retrospect he was rather proud of the adventure.

'Why? What was wrong with it?' asked a villager.

'We had nothing to eat for *two* days,' – Mr Bangun happily contemplated his brimming plate of curried rice, fish and vegetables.

Markus and I were quite satisfied with the results of our journey. We had found a few rhino tracks in the Bohorok River area, and even spotted a few orangs. There was one lone adult male, and later we met a pair – a female with a sub-adult consort male who displayed beautifully for us, shaking branches and letting the long hair on his back and arms wave about like a halo. We had found orang nests, even as high as 1800 metres above sea level. This was especially interesting, as orangs were previously believed to go no higher than 1500 metres; now we knew that they could cross ridges and high mountain cols that we had thought would be inaccessible to them.

In general, the upper Bohorok area seemed to be perfect orang country, with soft hills mantled in the most beautiful primary rain forest. Large fruit trees seemed to be plentiful, and the canopy stretched uninterrupted for mile after mile. It was certainly good country to bring orangs for resettlement – except for the difficulty of getting into it on foot. We shuddered to think of a caravan of bearers carrying crated orangs for four days up and down those slopes – it was quite impossible.

Helicoptering was the obvious way; indeed it was our only chance of using this splendid forest for resettlement. Markus had flown over the forest in helicopters with geological teams earlier in the year, and was impressed with the simplicity of these operations. So we had marked out a possible landing spot at Simpang Dua, the fork of the Bohorok. But helicopter flights were expensive. It would be some time yet before we could think seriously of flying orangs to a new home in the forest between Bohorok and Kutacane.

Above: Monica Borner. *Below:* Regina Frey.

Opposite: The kitchen/laboratory. Monica examines blood samples while Regina thinks about the next meal. *Above:* Monica's room. *Overleaf:* The entrance. The notice board in two languages shows the links with the World Wildlife Fund and the Frankfurt Zoological Society.

EVERY VISITOR MUST BE ACCOMPANIED
BY A GAME RANGER

SE TIAP TAMU HARUS DISERTAI OLEH
PETUGAS STASION

Opposite: Suka learning to climb. *Above:* Little Mo testing the strength of a slender branch. *Overleaf:* Olip investigates Dieter Plage's cine camera.

8
Sightseers

It was about this time that we began to notice the sightseers. During the building period we had always had one or two local people wandering around the camp: now they started to appear in numbers. They were mostly from nearby villages, out for a day in the forest with a hope of seeing the orangs – or preferably, the orangs *and* the strange European women who looked after them – at the new station. Wumi appointed herself watch-dog, patrolling the station with a proprietorial air. Carefully, though none too diplomatically, she drew her own distinction between foreign and native visitors. She let the foreigners off with a bark, but tackled the Indonesians ferociously, growling with hair on end and snapping around their heels. Many of them stood rooted to the spot, not daring to move until we had called Wumi off and welcomed them. As time went on, her opportunities to play watch-dog increased, for the place began to swarm with visitors.

The reason was simple: the wildest rumours were circulating locally about goings-on at the station. We heard with interest, for example, that two European women were climbing around naked in the trees, teaching orangs how to be wild animals. Ultimately a headline in the local paper summed it up: '*Dua wanita tarzan* – the two Tarzan girls'. That sparked off even more sightseers – enough to convince us that we had a problem on our hands, and would have to do something about it.

Clearly we couldn't allow crowds of visitors to wander unsupervised through the station; it would just be asking for trouble. And we had to keep people away from the quarantine cages, where they might prove a possible source of infection for the animals. But were we justified in trying to discourage visitors from coming to see us at all? Wouldn't the work benefit in the long run from the interest of outsiders – especially the local people, whose country we were in, whose orangs we were handling, and on whose co-operation the success of the scheme ultimately depended?

It wasn't a simple problem and we certainly didn't solve it in a single brilliant exchange of ideas. There were too many angles to it for that. Quite apart from the risk of infection, visitors would make the work of rehabilitation more difficult, for the orangs would probably find this human company entertaining, and be more inclined to stay around the station. Visitors meant more work too, for they had to be controlled; that meant that one of us or our staff would always have to be on hand to escort them. And we couldn't charge an entrance fee to defray expenses, as we might have done in Europe; these were poor people with little to offer but their interest and – possibly – their goodwill.

'We must be clear in our own minds what this project is really about', said Regina. 'If it's just a matter of getting a few dozen captured orangs back to the wild as quickly as possible, then visitors are a drawback.'

'But does this whole rehabilitation business make sense if we don't explain to people why we are doing it? After all they are the ones who catch the orangs, and buy and sell them; we'll be relying on them to pass the word around, and they have to understand in the first place what the project is about.'

'Quite so', Regina agreed. 'If they think we are running this project just for our personal satisfaction, they are not so likely to be helpful. They may even get the idea of going out and catching orangs in the forest and bringing them in for us. . . .'

'So we should really be attracting visitors, and putting their curiosity to good use. They may come to gape at us and the orangs, but we'll put them in the picture about what we are doing with the orangs, and about the meaning of nature conservation and the role of the rain forest in general. . . .'

So our ideas developed over the months. We decided to accept the extra work and all the other problems involved, and gear ourselves to encouraging visitors. But we were fairly restrictive. We allowed visitors to enter the Reserve for only two hours each day – in fact only at the afternoon feeding time – when they were always accompanied by one of the orang keepers. We had to make sure that the visitors and orangs did not make direct contact. After a time, as we became more confident and more convinced of their value, we maintained the rules around the station but began printing and distributing leaflets, explaining what the project was about. This was something that Regina liked doing and did well: much of the educational and public relations development was due to her skill and enthusiasm. Later still we began to cast a wider net, wooing tourists with articles on the orang rehabilitation station, and circulating brochures to hotels and travel agencies. For by now we had made up our minds: we wanted to do more with the station than simply rehabilitate orangs, and make a local population conservation-conscious. We hoped now to encourage a stream of visitors from the local population, as well as from the towns, and even from abroad, to help spread the word about nature conservation in the rain forest to a wider public, and publicize the related problem of the destruction of the forest at the same time.

Among our earliest visitors were some who, by a curious chance, were able to help us considerably. Returning home from the forest one afternoon I was met by an excited Regina. 'We have visitors – important visitors – come back quickly', she said. As we hurried along the track between bamboos and ferns, Regina told me that a dozen or so Indonesian ladies, all of them

wives of important officials, had come to see us. They had made
the expedition to find out for themselves the truth about the
rumour that two European girls were living alone with the apes.
These were sophisticated townsfolk, who had travelled a long
way to see us. Regina had set tea before them and hastened to
collect me from the forest.

Our little sitting-room was bursting with colourful, cheerful,
young-to-middle-aged Indonesian ladies, all drinking tea,
nibbling nuts and chatting amongst themselves. Regina introduced me to the most senior of them – Ibu Alex, the wife of the
Commander-in-Chief of Sumatra. She in turn introduced her
friends, who were mainly the wives of police, army and government officials responsible for the North Sumatra Province.
Their visit was a complete surprise. The path from Bukit
Lawang was still rough, and there was no boat at the river
crossing. Unsuitably shod in delicate sandals, and unaccus-
tomed to long walks in rough country, they had nevertheless
coped bravely. To cross the river they had linked arms and
formed a chain, supported by their accompanying soldiers at
either end. The chain had broken and some had got soaked and
lost their shoes – but here they were, chattering happily about
the orangs and asking for details of ourselves and our work.

They were friendly and interested, wanting to know how we
liked Indonesia, and how we managed to live in the forest. We
explained as best we could. Perhaps what surprised them most
was that, although I was married, Markus my husband stayed
away for months at a time. To them this seemed a strange sort of
arrangement, and not at all what marriages were really about.

Finally we set off up the hill to see the orangs at their
afternoon feed. In their soft little sandals with gilded straps and
thin soles, our guests slithered on the steep path. Out of condition, they puffed and panted, frequently pausing for breath and
to wipe their streaming brows. During one such pause, Ibu
Alex said something which almost took *my* breath away.

'I can understand your liking orangs', she panted. 'I have two pet ones myself, and I'm very fond of them. You must come and see them one day.' At the next pause, a little higher up the path, she continued: 'In Java, where my home is, I keep another two. I once had four there, but one died and I gave one to the zoo.' This was intriguing news. Keeping orangs in captivity had been illegal for 40 years or more. Yet here was the wife of the Commander-in-Chief happily talking of her own pet captive orangs. 'Yes,' chimed in one of her friends – the wife of a chief of police, 'my orang's a darling too. Sometime when you are in Binjai you must come and see us, and tell us how to improve her cage.'

We had known for some time that the law about keeping orangs captive was often flouted by wealthy people throughout the country. We knew, too, that there was nothing we could do about it officially; the PPA was helpless where influential officials were concerned, and it was not our job to reform Indonesian society – we could only protect its orangs if and when we saw chances. As we reached the rehabilitation cages the germ of an idea struck me. There was a glint in Regina's eye too as we exchanged glances – perhaps it had struck her as well? If we could persuade these people to give up their orangs to the station . . .? It would need a lot of diplomacy and very careful negotiation, but it might set a useful trend in our favour. I prepared to tackle Ibu Alex.

Our six orangs, now well advanced in rehabilitation and living free during the day, swooped down from the tree-tops as the party arrived. For once they played their part as diplomats and negotiators; they ignored the visitors completely, tucking into the bananas that Dekking had brought and squabbling cheerfully among themselves in unashamed greed. Even Cabe showed more interest in the bananas than in us – for which we were grateful. Then they swarmed back into the trees with cheeks and tummies bulging, swinging and trapezing in an unrehearsed ballet above our heads. The ladies were entranced, and so was I. Nothing I could have said, diplomatically or otherwise, would have made the point as clearly as the apes had made it themselves.

Our visitors' first responses – to move in and pet the lovable, furry creatures – had been checked by my stern warning: 'No touching please – the orangs are getting used to being wild.' Then they relaxed and watched, fascinated by the scene in front of them. Perhaps for the first time they were seeing, as free independent creatures, the animals they had known only as captives. Perhaps they could see, far more clearly than we had explained, why two Swiss girls chose to live in the jungle, even enjoying it, perhaps, too, why an international wildlife organization wanted to protect the orangs that they took so much for granted as pets.

We had no means of telling just then; our visitors twittered gaily on the path back to the station, and Ibu Alex and the wife of the police chief pressed on us invitations to visit them. But we felt our policy of encouraging visitors was vindicated, and events proved us right. It took time, but ultimately we gained several captive orangs, as well as a deal of friendship and goodwill, from that afternoon's tea-party with the officials' wives. It may well have marked a turning point in our whole rehabilitation programme.

9
Problem Children

Word soon got around that Bohorok station was open for the reception of orangs. There was no immediate parade of conscience-stricken owners beating their way to our door, but we were pleasantly surprised when the first voluntarily-donated orang came our way. One day in Medan, Markus was approached by a German. 'I have a little orang at home, and need to give it away soon because we are leaving. I've heard of your project, but I don't really know . . . would it perhaps be better to give the orang to a zoo? He's a real pet, and maybe the forest is dangerous if he doesn't know his way around.'

To reassure him, Markus invited him to visit us and see the project for himself. He came one weekend with his wife, his young son and his orang, staying overnight and having a good look round. The orang, Olip, was a hefty little chap, 18 months old, with long thick hair and eyes that opened like saucers in astonishment. The family parted with him sadly, cheering up when we promised to keep him in the house at first, so that he could gradually get used to his new life.

Olip settled quickly. Though deprived of his mother at an early stage, he had clearly been given all the love and attention he needed by kind foster-parents; happy and relaxed, he showed none of the anxieties that still bedevilled Cabe from time to time. Our company was always welcome, but he was quite content to be left on his own as well. Olip particularly enjoyed playing with Wumi in the grass in front of the house, seizing her tightly with all four paws while she gently nibbled her tummy with her teeth. We liked Olip. He turned out to be one of our most stupid orangs. Though he was friendly and funny, it took him longer than anyone else to understand what he was supposed to do. But he was a simple, honest creature without guile, and always good company.

Ilu was a different proposition altogether. His name means 'pitiable', and he was brought to us one night in a box, one of two babies snatched by the PPA from poachers in a village near Kandang. When we opened the box, a whining, wailing creature stretched out his arms towards us, a creature with the thin, sad face of an old man and a tiny emaciated body. He was covered with dung and the first thing he needed was a hot bath. In the box with him was the second ape, even tinier and – perhaps mercifully – now dead. The bottom of the box was a mess of dung, unpeeled green bananas and rice – not the best food for two small animals that should still have been living mainly on their mothers' milk.

Judging by his teeth, Ilu was 7 or 8 months old, but he weighed no more than 3 pounds – as much as he'd weighed at birth. Ilu was almost hairless, so we made him clothes to keep him warm. Jackets for new-born human babies were much too big, so I cut the foot off a wool stocking: the stocking leg made an excellent sleeveless pullover, and the heel a little cap for his bald head. He slept in a basket padded with cloths. To save having to wash his bedding all the time, we made him waterproof pants from a plastic bag and an old handkerchief, with absorbent tissues for nappies.

Feeding him was a struggle from the start. We tried giving him baby milk, but he spat it out, screaming and being sick. In desperation we resorted to force, using a plastic syringe to pour a trickle of diluted milk down him every 10 minutes or so. After a few hours he began to suckle feebly, and we felt there was hope for him. Like undernourished humans, Ilu had great difficulty holding down food of any kind. We made up mixtures of rice water, milk powder and bananas, sometimes with a little yolk of egg, sometimes with vitamins. It was always a great event when he retained a meal without vomiting or diarrhoea. Then he began to drink from the bottle, but in such tiny amounts that feeds had to be repeated every 2 hours. He established this timetable himself, simply by starting to cry every 2 hours, day and night. We took turns to look after him at night, so that at least one of us got some sleep.

Like an alarm clock he clamoured at the side of my bed, promptly on the second hour. His thin, wailing voice drilled into my sleep, starting a sequence of practical thoughts – find the matches, light the kerosene lamp, milk bottle – nappies. . . I would waken to feel my hand clutched by four tiny paws, and a soft, insistent mouth nuzzling my fingers for milk. Lifting him out of his basket, I'd feed him the bottle which had been keeping warm beside the bed. Often his nappy needed changing: sometimes we'd have to walk to the bathroom to wash him and sprinkle baby powder on his sore bottom, before settling him again.

Unlike a human baby, which lies fairly still when you put it down, Ilu hung on and climbed. It was in his nature to clutch at a mother, so he clutched at us relentlessly. So we put a strong lid on the basket and tied it down. Ilu managed to live with this, sleeping peacefully as long as the lid was tied down tightly. But if he could get a hand or arm out, he stayed awake crying. So our night's sleep depended not just on Ilu's appetite, but on our ability to tie a sound knot in a piece of string. Usually the drink made him sleepy and he would let himself be put back in his basket without a struggle. He'd sleep soundly for 2 hours, and off we would go again.

Through Ilu we established a firm and very beneficial friendship with Dr Kosasih and his wife, who lived in Medan. Dr Kosasih, a research haematologist, as well as a medical practitioner, was working on aspects of hepatitis, a disease not uncommon among men and animals in Indonesia. He first contacted us with a request that he be allowed to investigate our orang's blood, and he visited the station to collect blood samples during Ilu's long period of critical illness. Before leaving, Dr Kosasih looked Ilu over and gave him an iron injection which he felt would improve the little ape's general condition. That night, however, Ilu's sickness and diarrhoea increased in an alarming way, and I determined to take him down to Medan as soon as possible, to get Dr Kosasih's advice.

As a guest of the Kosasih's Ilu pulled round under treatment and soon recovered considerably from his upset. Meanwhile he acquired a yellow wool baby-jacket several sizes too big, a gift from Mrs Kosasih, whose own children had outgrown it many years before. Word quickly got around that the Kosasihs had an unusual little visitor, and many of their friends came to see Ilu. That gave us a chance to tell them about the station and the ideas behind what we were doing there. It was important to stop people getting the impression that we were no more than foster mothers for baby orangs. As a result of these contacts we had several new visitors at the station, and widened the circle of people on the lookout for orangs in captivity. Most important of all, friendship and co-operation grew up between Dr and Mrs Kosasih and the Station. He checked with interest samples of blood and faeces from all our new arrivals, and was always ready to help, whether it was the orangs or – very occasionally – ourselves who needed his treatment.

After 10 weeks of ups and downs Ilu was finally on the mend. His weight was almost back to normal, and he was developing well. Like Rimba, the first infant who died, and Cabe who was alive and improving steadily, Ilu taught us just a little more about handling baby orangs. From these experiences we established a routine which looked after both the physical and the psychological needs of the ones who followed.

Up to about 2 years old we kept them close to us. Throughout the day they swung and clambered in a playpen by the house – a pen made of strong wooden stakes, closed at the top to keep them in. In this they ate, rested, and played at nest-making with branches and fronds. Several times a day they got milk from the bottle, with fruit, fresh vegetables and young leaves. Often we opened the lid of the pen, leaving them free to practise climbing in the trees round our house. A few preferred the safety of the pen. We had to lift them out and hang them onto small trees, trying to persuade them that climbing is fun. Usually they would tumble down shrieking and have to be put back in the trees again and again. In time they would realize that we were always within sight and earshot, even when they were climbing, then they were happy to climb and practise their gymnastics on the trees, and stay away from the playpen for longer and longer.

Every day we took them with us on a short walk in the forest, so they would get used to its smells and sounds. We played with them, letting them sit on our laps while we read. In the evening we took them into the house for a quarter of an hour. This they seemed to like best of all. We were always within easy reach, and there were all kinds of wonderful things to investigate and keep them busy. We didn't have time to get bored either, when three small apes went exploring in our 70 square feet of living room. While one despatched a quiet bit of business under the table, the second shinned up the bookcase, to hang by one hand from the top shelf and chew the edges of the Indonesian dictionary. Then the third upset a chair and practised advanced climbing techniques around the legs, or drummed unmusically with his fist on the tin medicine chest. Always they kept one eye on us, returning to our laps every few minutes for a hug and a bit of stroking. When the party was over, they would get a biscuit or a favourite fruit, and be put to bed in wooden nursery boxes beside the house. Apart from a soft, contented smacking of lips no more would be heard: they'd snuggle down in their blankets and sleep soundly till morning.

We reared seven small orangs on this system without any of them becoming neurotic or difficult. At about 2 years they would spend their nights in a cage in the forest and their days in the open with other orangs or climbing around on their own. It was they who ultimately cut down contact with us; less and less often wanting to sit on our lap, and eventually coming within reach only at feeding time. The practice we followed was designed to match closely what we felt were the natural needs of the young apes at different stages, and we were always glad to see them graduating from one stage to the next, eventually achieving full independence.

Even when it took years for our small orangs to reach this final stage, bringing them up was a very rewarding task. Though we knew little of child-rearing at the time, we have since had opportunities to talk to child psychiatrists and psychologists about our problem babies, and found a great deal of common ground. Human children react to harmful environmental influences – isolation and withdrawal of maternal love, for example – very much as our young orangs were reacting as a result of their traumatic capture and isolation in captivity. Just like Cabe and our other deprived babies, neglected and lonely children shy away from contacts. They sit around on their own, hugging themselves and rocking their bodies too and fro, becoming either lethargic and indifferent or impossibly demanding. An established treatment for such children, we learned, is "mothering" – building up a close relationship with them, rocking them on one's lap, giving way to their demands, even bottle-feeding them like babies if that is what they seem to need. This was just what we, acting instinctively, had done with Cabe. Sadly, it is usually the case that disturbed human children take much longer than small orangs to overcome their psychological difficulties, and many never recover – even with the kindest and most understanding treatment in later life.

Nobody has yet seen the birth of a young orang in the wild. Presumably the mothers produce their young in the safety of the nest, where we are least likely to see them. We had no mothers with very young babies at Bohorok, but I did manage to watch one during visits to Ketambe, some time after Ilu's arrival. The mother was Binjai, a young orang whom the Rijksens had released after rehabilitation. Some years after her release, during which she had been quite a regular visitor to the feeding site, she appeared again at the station with a tiny infant, obviously no more than 3 or 4 days old. Binjai seemed to be a relaxed, happy mother; used to the company of humans, she did not in the least mind being watched and followed through the forest. So I visited Ketambe a month after the birth, and again every 5 or 6 weeks for the first 5 months, to see what she did with the baby, and monitor its development.

Orang babies weigh 3 or 4 pounds at birth. They have long, lean arms and lanky legs – they are not at all plump and round like human babies – and their fingers and toes are strong enough for effective gripping right from the start. At birth the body is already covered with reddish-orange hair, thick and long on the back but much thinner in front. Almost immediately after birth the baby clings face-inwards to its mother's body, so the mother's warmth passes readily to it through the bare abdominal skin.

Binjai's baby was about 5 weeks old when I first saw it. A tiny, spidery creature less than a foot long, it seemed to spend most of its time asleep, clinging close to its mother's side with fingers and toes knotted firmly into the fur of her belly and back. When it awoke, it would weave its head slowly from side to side, tracking until its mouth came into contact with one of her nipples. Then it would start to suck; from the movements of its upper lip I could see that it usually drank only for a few minutes at a time. If the baby was too low to find the nipple, Binjai would hitch it up to the right level with her arm. Except for this, she seemed to make little response to her offspring during the first few weeks. There were times, indeed, when she seemed to have forgotten altogether about it. But watching closely, I saw that she never exposed it unnecessarily to danger. Her posture, for example constantly offered the clinging baby support. She might hang from a branch with both hands and one foot, but the baby was always held safely between her raised thigh and belly. Hanging sideways from one arm and one leg, she contrived to have the baby lying along her flank. All her movements were leisurely and controlled, so the baby was seldom shaken or bounced.

At that time Binjai was accompanied by Bumi, a young male of about 3 years old whom she had adopted a year earlier. Despite the little one clinging constantly to her she still managed to romp with Bumi, who was seldom far from her. She was patient with him, letting him suckle from her now and then, or snatch bananas from her hand or mouth. She played with him a lot, and let him sleep in the nest with her and the baby. When they moved off from the feeding place Bumi would often cling to her, just like the baby, and she would have to climb with one on either flank. Bumi was always interested in the baby, though I never saw him hold or fondle it.

As the weeks passed the baby became more active. Whenever it lay safely on top of her it would loosen its hold; through binoculars I could often see its hands and feet waving free and exploring Binjai's fur. But the moment she gave even a hint of changing her position, the baby's hands clutched hard at her coat again. After large meals or long sessions of playing with Bumi, Binjai would often withdraw to the broad fork of a branch or make herself a small nest, leaving Bumi to play on his own. There she would spend a while resting and paying more attention to the baby. Sometimes she pulled it away from her and held it in front of her face at arms' length; the little one would cry, with its feet searching shakily for a hold. Again she might lie on her back with the baby crawling uncertainly over the dome of her belly. Then she would pull it hard against her face, closing her lips round the baby's mouth or forehead. It looked as though she was sucking it gently, while the young one in turn sucked hard at its mother's lower lip.

Later still the baby often seemed like a toy to her; though Binjai was clearly a tender and caring mother, she sometimes gave it what seemed to me a fairly rough time. She would pluck it loose from her fur and hold it nonchalantly in one hand, the baby yelling and floundering helplessly with legs and arms pedalling frantically. She would sneak a quick glance at it, then look away into the distance while the infant's shrieks redoubled. Finally she would draw it back to her breast and hug it tenderly. Sometimes she rocked the baby to and fro between her thighs, with its belly rubbing against her genitals; she didn't seem in the least concerned at its complaints. But in all the time I watched her she never abandoned the infant or left it to cry on its own. It was never out of contact with her, and never for more than a minute away from the reassuring warmth of her body.

As the baby grew larger and stronger, Binjai became less constrained in her movements. She would wrestle with Bumi and with other orangs at the feeding table, falling forward and rolling almost as though the infant was not there. But whether she was hanging upside down by her feet, or clambering actively with arms and legs, the young one clung hard. It still seemed to sleep for much of the day, but it never let go.

I didn't see as much of Binjai and her family as I would have liked, but their closeness as a unit was impressive. I saw for myself how completely dependent was an orang infant for the first 2 or 3 years of its life. And I realized how much close attention we would need to give our own foster-babies if they were to grow into anything like normal adults.

Binjai's responses to Bumi were in a way just as interesting as her dealings with the baby, though I had seen other examples of this kind of behaviour between young and adopting adults. Sometimes in the early hours of the morning, when I was wearily tending a squalling infant, I thought how convenient it would be if we could persuade some of our adult or sub-adult

95

females to adopt our orphans. But unfortunately it wouldn't have worked. Though an adolescent female might readily take up a 9-months-old baby, and the baby might happily cling to her, there would still be a lot missing from the relationship. The female would have no milk, and might not know the trick of feeding the infant, at least in part, on chewed leaves. She might well grow tired of the whole business long before the infant could cope for itself. If she took it off to the forest we would never know whether or not the experiment had worked; we could never be standing by with supplementary feeds or medicines should they be needed. The idea was tempting but we rejected it, and continued to play foster-mother ourselves.

We did, however, introduce the infants to the older orangs at the feeding place, where they were always objects of a general kindly interest. Sitting on the cage with an infant on my knee, I would usually be approached by two or three of the orangs. One might stretch out his hand, touch the infant lightly and then sniff his fingertips – and inelegant but genuine expression of interest. Another would tug gently at a foot or hand, or even try to take the infant away from me, but always in a restrained, kindly way, without any indication of aggression or jealousy.

Adolescent females were particularly intrigued by the babies. As they might normally have remained with their mothers for quite some time after the appearance of a younger brother or sister, and perhaps have handled the growing infant them-selves, we sometimes gave them a baby orang to play with. This always delighted them, and it meant that they would not altogether lack the experience of getting to know and handle an infant before being faced for the first time with one of their own. I knew that many young mother apes in zoos rejected or killed their own young – especially their firstborn – perhaps as a result of being brought up in isolation, or in the company only of other young apes, without having a chance to handle a baby before their own was born. If the problem existed among our own orangs, this might be a good way of heading it off.

We ran a series of experiments, putting a small baby in the cage of a young female and withdrawing out of sight. We were never out of hearing – like anxious mothers at a kindergarten, we stayed in the wings in case we were needed in a hurry. We knew, too, that the babies would never even look at the adults so long as we were around. The babies usually began by clinging to the bars of the cage, sometimes for several sessions, until the gentle interest of the adult won them over. The adults – without exception – approached with tact and kindly intent, and always ended up by playing happily with the youngster after a few sessions. Adults and babies both benefited, and we learned one more delightful fact about our orangs – they seemed universally fond of their children.

No therapy of ours could improve the lot of Rambong, an adult female whose whole life since infancy had been spent in conditions of isolation and deprivation. Through local friends we found Rambong in the possession of a plantation foreman, who was only too glad to get her off his hands when the PPA called. Her home was a packing case $1\frac{1}{2}$ metres long and 1 metre across. Floor, walls and ceiling were of solid boards; the box had no windows, and offered no opportunities for climbing – Rambong even had difficulty in stretching or moving about inside it. In this dungeon she had spent the last 8 years of her life. There was a hole in the wall as big as a fist, for rice to be thrown through now and again, and from time to time her owner stuck a hose into the box to wash it down inside.

It was the old story. Bought as a baby, Rambong had originally been bottle-fed and cosseted, though not for long. When her owners couldn't be bothered with her any more, she was relegated to the box and kept there, with a casual indifference and ignorance we found all too common among the owners of wild animal pets. There were no further contacts made for her, human or animal. There was no sun – nothing to see, to clutch at or play with, nothing to occupy a lively mind and body. After

8 years of neglect she was a cowering wreck; like a dirty, unkempt bundle, she huddled on a block in one corner of her box, clutching her shoulders with crossed arms. Saliva dribbled from her half-open mouth. Her coat, filthy with dung, was matted about her, and scrawny arms and legs testified to appalling lack of condition. Rambong was indeed physically ill, but she was mentally crippled too, beyond anything we had seen before in the apes we had handled.

It hardly surprised us that she would not leave her box when we went to collect her. It was her world; she knew no other, and we had to drag her bodily out of it to get her into a travelling crate. Once in the crate, with the lid firmly down, she relaxed again, wrapped in the familiar darkness of a closed box. Whenever we looked in during the journey she crouched silently, with head down and hands firmly grasping her shoulders. At the station we placed the crate in a quarantine cage and opened the lid, but she made no attempt to leave it. After 2 days we had to drag her out yet again, this time into a roomy cage where the fresh air, the light and the sounds of the forest surrounded her. Rambong lay motionless where we had left her, crouched on her stomach in the farthest corner. It was some hours before she dared to move. Then she crawled on her belly, resting her head on her folded arms and pushing herself forward with her feet. Several days passed before she trusted herself to stand upright, or move normally from one corner of her new quarters to another.

In time Rambong got used to her new cage and to the sights, sounds and smells of Bohorok. No longer dragging herself on her stomach, she even began to climb. At first she climbed always in a circle, in a strange, ritualized way we had never seen before. Her hands and feet clutched the same points on the bars, which became worn and polished where she touched them. It was weeks before she grew more adventurous and began to climb and swing freely about her cage. To us she was unresponsive. Only her new diet seemed to please her – after 8 years of rice she ate fruit and leaves and drank enriched milk greedily, though only in small amounts at a time.

Finally her quarantine period was over and, after a spell in the rehabilitation cages, we let her go free. The open door of the cage meant nothing to her; for the third and final time we had to drag her bodily out. We half expected that, outside the familiar four walls, she would once again go down on her belly and revert to crawling. But that phase was over – the spell was broken. Slowly, jerkily, with painfully clumsy movements, she started to climb the tree nearest to the cage door. She spent the rest of the day circling carefully from one tree to the next above the rehabilitation cages, coming down at feeding time to collect the food we laid out for her. Then she climbed again, finally coming down to sleep in the open on top of the cage. Neither at that time nor later could we persuade her to enter a cage or a box again.

Although she sometimes made use of the old nests in the trees nearby, Rambong continued to use the top of the cage as her sleeping quarters. Her huddled figure became a familiar sight at feeding time and in the evenings. She responded strangely to the other apes, grooming the small ones endlessly until they were free of every tiny particle of scurf, though her own fur remained matted and unkempt. On the other hand, she seemed frightened of any orang older than about 4 years, keeping out of their way. In spite of her special diet she never put on weight, remaining thin and scrawny; soaked by every storm, she nearly always seemed to suffer from colds, which may have dragged her down physically. We lost her eventually after an attempt, perhaps misguided, to cure her with medication. Rambong resented the handling and disappeared almost immediately afterwards. It is difficult to imagine that she ever recovered – mentally or physically – to a stage where she could care for herself. We assume that she died in the forest a few days later.

10
Rehabilitation

For the first few months after opening the station we took in orangs as they came. A few were brought in from private sources, and more came to us from the PPA as Gersom Sinaga and his colleagues stepped up their campaign in the north and west. The cages filled and emptied as a succession of young, healthy juveniles passed quickly through to freedom. Infants and difficult cases took longer, but they too made steady progress. We were never short of animals, never casting about to see where the next ones were coming from, and never at a loss for something to do.

But our thoughts returned constantly to the conversation we had had with Ibu Alex and her friends. How could we get our hands on the captive orangs of these pleasant, influential people? Could we manage by tact what the PPA would never hope to achieve by official methods? Renewing Ibu Alex's acquaintance – taking up her kind invitation to tea – this was an obvious first step. So Regina and I tidied ourselves up one hot afternoon and drove into Medan, for a social call at the official residence of General Alex, the Commander-in-Chief of Sumatra. Ibu Alex made us welcome. Cool and elegant in European clothes, with a high hair-do, she gave us tea and showed us round the garden. We met Sera, her pet orang – a lively, light tan-coloured female, 5 or 6 years old. Radiant with health and zest, Sera swung cheerfully in an airy cage, close to a pair of very noisy Alsatians in a corner of the garden.

'She's been in captivity about a year', said Ibu Alex, 'my husband was given her by a junior officer. She's rather shy, but has an insatiable appetite'.

We saw that a neighbouring cage was occupied by a second orang, as different from Sera as chalk from cheese. 'He's called Gareng,' said Ibu Alex. 'I got him just a few days ago from a soldier: he gave him to me because the poor thing seemed ill, and needed treatment.'

'Gareng' means clown, but this was the saddest clown we had ever seen. About 10 years old, he was desperately thin, dishevelled and almost completely paralysed. Crouching in one corner of the cage, he followed us only with his eyes, keeping upright by propping himself on his elbows. His lower lip hung uselessly down, and his dark face looked grey with exhaustion. When we spoke to him, he answered with tiny, willing squeaks that died in his throat. 'The problem is, poor Gareng has diarrhoea all the time. I've had the vet to him. He gave him injections against amoebic dysentery, but since he had the injections his paralysis is much worse. He can't move his legs at all.

We were appalled at the thought of how this animal had managed to get into such a state. The soldier, said Ibu Alex, had had Gareng for years. Previously stationed in Kalimantan, he bought the orang as a baby and brought it with him to Sumatra. We were not surprised to hear this; Gareng's dark coat and bare face showed him to be of the Bornean sub-species. The soldier admitted that he had kept the animal chained for a long time because, as it got bigger, it became strong enough to break out of any cage; the chain was the only way of keeping it under control. We wondered whether Gareng was simply paralysed from muscular deterioration and stiff joints – products of long imprisonment – or whether he had suffered polio into the bargain.

Ibu Alex seemed fond of her orangs, and somehow the

question of our acquiring them did not arise at this meeting. We talked for a time, promised to drop in again, and returned to Bohorok.

Back in Medan a few weeks later, we heard that the General's wife was hoping to see us, and we hastened over to the Residency. Ibu Alex welcomed us warmly again, and led us into the garden. Sera still swung excitedly in her cage, healthy and cheerful as ever, but Gareng's condition was worse – much worse, and Ibu Alex was worried. 'I've been thinking it over, and I really would like to give you my orangs', she said suddenly. 'Why should they spend their lives sitting in a cage – they'd have a much better time in the forest. Perhaps they could even marry and have children there.'

It was a happy thought. We were surprised and absolutely delighted. Though Gareng obviously had many problems to solve (and many difficulties to overcome before thinking of marriage), Sera would be no trouble at all; we could see her passing very quickly through our hands and taking her rightful, natural place in the forest. And what a splendid example it would be to other pet owners if the Commander-in-Chief's wife . . . But Ibu Alex hadn't finished.

'I'm going to tell all my friends who've got orangs about your work', she promised. 'The Chief of Police of Sumatra has a sweet little orang that goes for a ride every day with his son on a bicycle. And the Chief of Police of North Sumatra Province has two females – he's had them a long time. One is grown-up now and he was thinking of trying to breed from her . . . but I'll persuade him to give you them both. And tomorrow I'll ring up the wife of the Bupati [Head of District] at Binjai. She has a young female orang that she might give you. . . .'

It was a tremendous breakthrough. If all these officials could be persuaded to give us their orangs of their own free will, it couldn't fail to have an effect on their subordinates too. It might just become the fashion to support nature conservation and orang protection, instead of keeping wild animals as pets in the garden. We might even . . . but these were day-dreams. First, we had Sera and poor, sad Gareng to deal with.

Ibu Alex happily agreed to keep Sera for a few days longer, while we coped with Gareng. But coping with Gareng was not a simple matter. Back at Bohorok his condition deteriorated, and we were afraid that he would die on our hands. It soon became clear that only first-class medical treatment would save him. By chance we had met and made friends with a surgeon in Medan – Dr Erwin – and to him I took Gareng. Dr Erwin gave him the course of treatment that eventually saved his life.

We immobilized Gareng with elastic bandages on a lattice-work stretcher, so that we could treat him over a long period without his struggling or interfering. Dr Erwin introduced a saline drip, to give back some of the liquid and salts that Gareng was continually losing through his diarrhoea. As he refused all food and drink, we fed a stomach tube in through his nose and introduced into him strengthening milk-based liquids, and medicines to cure his amoebic dysentery.

I stayed at the doctor's house for about a week with Gareng, treating him as Dr Erwin directed. By then the diarrhoea was conquered, but Gareng had developed bed-sores – ulcers on his back from being fastened too long to the stretcher. To relieve Dr Erwin I took the patient to some other friends of ours – Frits and Riek Janssen – who lived on a plantation close by. Riek, who had trained as a nurse, tended Gareng for a further six weeks, eventually restoring him to a reasonable state of health – far better health than he had probably known for many a long year.

Sera and Gareng came home to Bohorok together in July 1974, 4 months after our first meeting with Ibu Alex. With them came Pandi, the young female whom Ibu Alex had pro-mised to wheedle away from her friend the Bupati's wife. Sera and Pandi, bouncing with health and vitality and none the worse for captivity, passed quickly through the various stages of rehabilitation, soon joining the afternoon tea-parties of free-living orangs at the feeding place. Gareng, now strong and wiry but still convalescent, struggled gamely to overcome his paralysis. Climbing persistently, with immense difficulty and legs dangling uselessly, he first got back the partial use of his hands and arms. Then gradually the muscles of his legs and back improved a little too; his self-confidence returned in stages, and eventually he felt safe enough to play somewhat shakily in the trees with the younger orangs who were his daily companions. He was much in demand at the nursery – a gentle, kindly uncle to the little ones, always happy to join in the fun, but never grasping or biting too hard.

As Gareng played in the tree-tops, we remembered his awful condition only six months before. We blessed Ibu Alex for giving him to us, and silently thanked our medical friends for the miracle of his recovery.

Few of the animals we recovered from captivity gave us any thing like the troubles and anxieties of Gareng. Many were 'normal'; though chained or confined in cages, they had been petted as infants and cherished as juveniles, and had not lost the skills or the sense of enquiry that carry an orang through its daily life. During the first year at Bohorok we worked out a routine for handling these normal animals – a routine that could be applied, with only slight variation, to many of the juveniles and adolescents that passed through Bohorok.

Pesek ('flat-nose') was one such animal. Regina found him in the town of Lhok Seumawe, where she had stopped off over-night on the road to Banda Aceh. Making friends with local youngsters, she told them where she came from and what she was doing in Sumatra. Then one lad, the son of the village policeman, told her of a captive orang: it belonged to the head of the local Immigration Office, and Regina went round to his house that evening to negotiate for it. The officer was out, but his wife introduced her to Pesek – a smashing, powerful male about 5 years old, in a big wooden cage. Pesek was a family pet and obviously loved, but Regina sensed trouble. He was healthy, well-fed and very strong: soon he would be far too strong for a wooden cage in a small village garden.

She saw the Immigration Officer in his office the following morning. The interview got off to a bad start: he wanted to know all about her and why, as a visitor to Sumatra, she hadn't been to see him before. Regina kept cool and explained that she lived in another province, where the immigration people had all the information they needed. That satisfied his official dignity and he became more friendly, ready to talk about orangs. It seemed he had applied to Jakarta for permission to keep one in captivity, so Pesek was legitimate and could not be confiscated. They parted on friendly terms, and Regina invited him to come and see us – and our orangs – whenever he was in Bohorok.

In July 1974 Regina was back in Lhok Seumawe, answering an urgent summons that came to her through the local PPA office. Her instinct was right. Fortified by good living, Pesek had grown even bigger and stronger, and was now almost out of control. Already he had broken several times from his cage, raising hell in neighbouring gardens and chicken runs, and the Head of Immigration wanted rid of him. For Pesek it was us, or confinement in one of the dreadful Sumatran zoos, or even an early grave. It was fortunate for him that Bohorok station existed, and doubly fortunate that Regina had made herself known in the town on her stop-over 6 months before.

We were standing on the river bank when Pesek arrived at Bohorok. The dug-out canoe swayed alarmingly on the way across the river as he pounded around in his travel crate. But Dekking managed the crossing without incident, and we carried the box to the quarantine cages. Every orang arriving at the Station had to start with a few weeks in quarantine. Having spent time in contact with humans and domestic animals, they might well have been carrying diseases and parasites: we had to be sure they were free from malaria, hepatitis, amoebic dysentery, tuberculosis and polio when they were set free in the forest. Illnesses like that, transmitted to wild orangs, might destroy an entire local population. We had before us the awful example described by Jane Goodall in her book *In the Shadow of Man*, when polio spread to the forest from an African village, killing and crippling numbers of wild chimpanzees. So Pesek temporarily exchanged one form of captivity for another.

He started by putting his cage through a stiff durability trial, gnawing and tearing at the timber beams, flinging himself against the walls with all his strength, using branches as levers to try to bend the iron bars. But the cage was new and strong and passed the test. Roof, floor and walls were all made of a grille of strong iron bars, inserted into a frame of hardwood beams. The bars gave the orangs a chance to climb, let in air and light, and were easy to clean. The whole cage stood on stilts, so that most of the dirt fell through the floor grating and could be cleared from outside. The roof was partly covered with boards to keep the rain out.

Pesek now had plenty of time to study his new environment and us – and we to study him. We soon realized that, demanding and cheeky as he might be, he was very good-hearted and good-humoured about it all. When we tried to scrape samples of dung from his floor to be analysed for parasites, Pesek would suddenly seize our arm with one hand, following rapidly with a second, third and fourth, and hanging on tight. With a mere two hands we stood no chance against his four: it didn't hurt, but it was time-wasting and we learnt to dodge when we could. As a rule he would just hang on tight and gaze at us with contentment until he found something more rewarding – like my pony-tail hair-do. Then he would make a grab at that. Sometimes we ducked in time; sometimes we needed the help of one or two others to get free. Very often a good talking-to would make him loosen his grip. But once I was right out of luck. Standing close to the bars, I was peering into the back corners of the cage when he suddenly made a grab at my shirt. Thin from frequent washing, the shirt tore: with a swing of his arm he ripped it completely away and waved it triumphantly like a banner. I had to abandon my work and rush home to make myself presentable.

Sometimes, however, it was Pesek who came off worst; for example, when we had to take blood samples or inoculate him. As soon as he stretched out an arm to catch hold of us, he was caught instead and had his arm pulled firmly outwards through the bars. Three or four men helped catch his other hand and feet and pull them out too, so he finished up pinioned against the grille, helpless and looking rather sorry for himself. But he was still powerful – it took a strong man on each of his limbs to hold him reasonably still in this position. Then the veins had to be found under the close hair and thick skin, and a blood sample drawn off with a hypodermic. Blood samples from the station were checked in Medan, both for general state of health and for specific diseases such as hepatitis and malaria. A succession of samples gave us a clear picture of the progress of our wards. In addition, all the apes were given a tuberculosis inoculation in the forearm. Worm powders and polio inoculations were given by mouth, liberally mixed with condensed milk; these Pesek ate enthusiastically, even licking the spoon clean and asking for more.

But not all the orangs were so obliging. Particularly among the little ones were some who refused all medicines on principle, and could not be tricked into taking them. Force was the only answer; we opened their mouths, poured the medicine in, and held their noses until everything had gone down, usually with much gurgling and spitting. But force could be used only on the babies – even a 3-year-old orang could clamp his jaws together so hard that we had to give up. If all else failed and further treatment was needed, we just had to resort to further injections, usually in the thigh.

Quite apart from these medical checkups, the quarantine period gave us a good opportunity to observe the animals and get to know them. As well as the frisky and pushful Pesek we had quiet, shy ones, who buried their heads in their arms and blinked hesitatingly at the ground, like shy children. We had neurotic apes who clutched themselves continuously, and others who went round and round in circles – apathetic ones who always sat on the same spot gazing into the distance, and over-anxious ones who shot backwards and forwards in their cage whenever anyone went near them. With the help of our observations in the quarantine period we could decide exactly how we were going to handle each individual animal later.

It became quite clear with Pesek that he would not be much of a problem, though we worried a little about the day he would be set free – free to come down from the tree-tops and become the station pest, tyrannising us all with his cheerful presence.

Before the animals were freed they had to be given the chance to have a good look at other orangs and the forest – often for the first time in many years – and to get used to the new environment. This seemed an important step on their way back to the wild: we had to be sure that they didn't rush crazily off into the forest, but would have a good look round first. But there was always one other small problem to be solved first – how to transfer them from the quarantine cages to the rehabilitation site 500 yards away in the forest.

It was a particular problem in the case of Pesek, who knew all about small crates and was far too cunning to get into one of his own free will. He was certainly too strong to be forced into one. We tried a ruse. I offered him a rice sack as a new toy. After submitting it to a brief examination, he climbed playfully into it. This was the moment we were waiting for. Before Pesek knew what was going on, the mouth of the sack was tied securely and the puffing Dekking was lugging 50 lbs of solid ape up the hill to the rehabilitation cage.

The roof of this cage served also as the feeding place for the free orang utans, so Pesek had plenty of company. This was his chance to get used gradually to freedom. He saw how the free orangs gathered morning and evening for feeding; he took in the sights and smells of the forest, heard the rustle of trees in the rain, the chirping of crickets and the calling of birds and apes. Every day in his cage he was given branches and twigs to practise nest-building. Also, for the first time, he was sharing his cage with another orang. Pandi, a female of about his own age, size and weight, had an exceptionally friendly and pleasant disposition. But Pesek wasn't ready for the close company of another orang – even Pandi. He kept his distance, and they never really played together. After Pesek had spent a couple of weeks in the rehabilitation cage, its door was opened. He and Pandi went out together into the forest, truly free for the first time.

At this critical point of their lives almost all captive orangs behave in the same way. They climb straight up the nearest tree within reach. Only the clumsy, over-cautious (or sometimes madly breakneck) climbing movements show that they have been shut up for a long time. Some hesitate and secure themselves at each new hold; others swing gaily from branch to branch like siamangs, or even venture in leaps from one tree to the next. Once in a while they come a cropper and hurt themselves, learning the hard way what would have come naturally to a young orang growing up in the wild. Luckily, serious accidents were rare, and their endless practice soon gave most of the apes the climbing expertise they needed.

Pesek climbed about for hours on his first day of freedom. He ate leaves, and built himself a first experimental nest. He did this in the time-honoured orang way, bending small branches towards himself, forcing them together, pressing them and stamping them in place with hands and feet. Standing in the middle of the nest and turning round and round, he stretched out his arm for small twigs, which he broke off and pushed into the nest. He would even leave the platform to get particularly large or soft leaves that were growing out of reach, using them to line his nest before lying down in it.

The nest finished, he lay in it luxuriously with only a hand or foot still to be seen over the edge. Nests provide comfort and shelter at night, as well as freedom from ground predators, so making a safe nest is an essential skill for any orang.

Towards late afternoon Pesek, like his comrades in rehabilitation, would start getting hungry. He had seen how the other orangs came back to the rehabilitation cage and climbed down onto its roof, along thick bars running from the nearby trees. There they sat waiting, chewing at leaves or a twig they had brought with them, and scratching themselves thoughtfully. When one turned his head and focused his gaze on the spot where the narrow footpath disappeared between the trees, there was a good chance he had heard Dekking's approach – that tea was on its way.

The tea-party was always a delight to watch, especially for our visitors. First, Dekking appears, carrying a large rucksack full of bananas on his back, a 2 gallon bucket full of milk in one hand, and in the other a broom made from the springy midribs of palm leaves. He swings the rucksack onto the roof of the cage and climbs up behind it, his bare feet gripping the bars of the grille. Dekking's arrival makes even Pesek chance his newly-found freedom. Like the rest of the mob, he comes slowly onto the roof to get his share of bananas and milk, still hesitant and shy in the new surroundings.

Only the small and undernourished animals get milk. Though all orangs are crazy about it they behave very well at the feeding station, even the ones who get none. It would be only too easy for one of them to snatch up the whole bucket, or to dispute with another who was drinking from his tin. But they wait their turn: generally the only signs of impatience are nervous scratching or hands waving nervously around in the air. Sometimes, however, it gets too much even for the patience of an orang. Then they take excited bites at their neighbours in the queue, or fling themselves down shrieking and kicking, hammering with their fists on the ground and banging their heads, like children in a fit of uncontrolled temper. These tantrums last no more than half a minute; then the animal is calm again. In the end each gets his share, and can stuff any gaps left in his belly with a surfeit of bananas.

The apes who are used to all this climb off again into the trees, some carrying a private store of bananas in their mouth or free hand. Dekking cleans the feeding place and the cage beneath it with his broom. Pesek lies flat on his back on top of the cage, with short legs doubled up and long arms akimbo. He seems to want to settle down for the night there. Two smaller orangs slink along the ground into the undergrowth. They have not yet had enough practice in nest-building and, like Pesek, will have to be rounded up to spend the night in the cage. Pesek offers no resistance to being shut in; probably all the excitements of the day have tired him out. If these three were to spend the night in the open they would be exposed to enemies: tigers or clouded leopards would make short work of them as they lay on the ground, easy to get at and sound asleep.

To begin with, most orang utans that have lived for years in cages find the forest strange, unfamiliar and sometimes even intimidating. Life on the station, with the noises of human activity and regular meals of bananas, might well seem a more attractive proposition for them than the mysterious, uncertain forest. But soon curiosity, and perhaps an appetite for a more varied diet, win them over, and off they go exploring. Pesek, who had spent most of his life in captivity, had a lot to learn before we could give him a certificate of competence for independent life in the wild.

The first lesson may seem simple enough, but in fact may be almost the hardest for them to learn. The message had to be got across to the young orang that he is a tree animal, and does not belong on the ground. He can of course climb – this is an innate behaviour pattern. But skilled climbing has to be acquired by experience and practice. The novel experiences of each new day in the forest have to be put together – how thick a branch must be to support, how much a trunk will bend, and the best way of getting from one tree to the next. These skills could be acquired only in the trees. Every time Pesek followed his old habits of a domestic garden pet and ran around on the ground, we took him to the nearest tree and made him climb up it, threatening him in his own idiom by waving branches and sticks at him. We sometimes had to do this several times an hour until he stayed where he belonged – in the tree.

At the same time we had to make Pesek understand that human beings were not the best playmates for him. Learning to keep away from humans would be absolutely essential to his survival in his coming life in the wild. Many captive orangs had a persistent, almost indestructible trust in human kindness, even those that had suffered most severely in the hands of their captors. Again and again they would try to clutch at us playfully, to run after us on the ground or to come straight up to us when they saw us. So we had to brush them off if they came too near, or even threaten them by shaking and throwing branches. We explained to visitors that on no account may they touch the orangs or play with them. Many thought us heartless for discouraging the approaches of the 'dear sweet creatures, who were so obviously in need of love' – as one visitor put it. Actually we found it hard to turn away when an orang stretched out a hand to us and pulled a funny face – much harder than to accept the invitation to play. But it was the only way we knew to convince the animals of the change that had come into their lives – that the future lay in relating to other apes of their own kind, and not to man. Combined with the freedom of life in the trees, the message was finally taken. Most of our apes eventually gave up their interest in unresponsive humans: as time went on they even became shy, avoiding accidental contacts with us at the feeding place and drawing back when we approached them.

To the relief of us all, Pesek got used to his new life in the trees more quickly than we had expected. Far from becoming the station pest, he stayed up near the feeding place and explored away from the houses, spending whole days and

Overleaf: Suka takes his pick of bananas on top of the cages. *Above:*
Regina collecting a pet orang.

Monica coaxing a pet orang off his perch at the drilling site.

Above: Preparing for bed in the quarantine cage. *Opposite:* A six-months-old orang sleeping after his medical treatment.

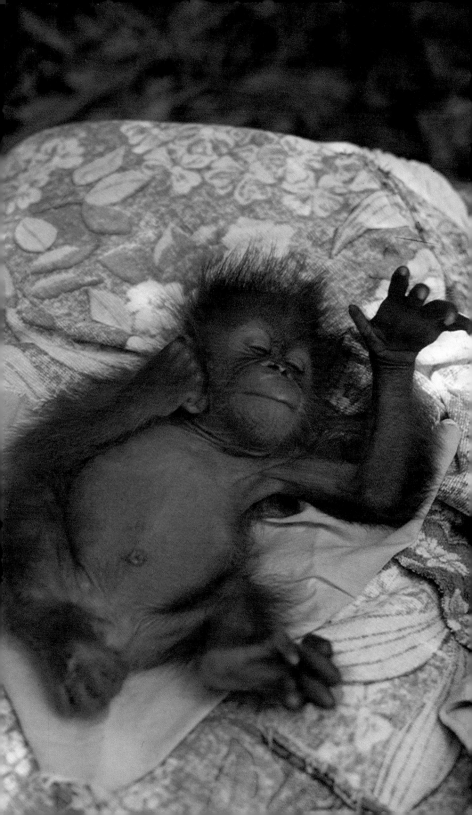

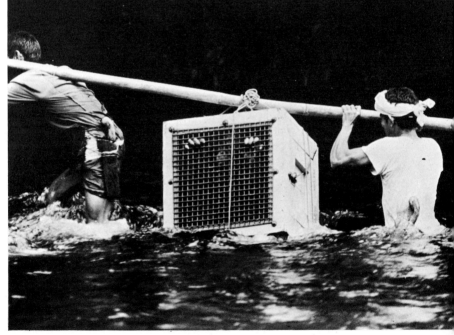

Opposite, above: Crossing the river with Ojuk in his crate. *Below:* Ojuk looks apprehensive as the water deepens. *Above:* Swept off their feet by the current, the bearers drop Ojuk in the water.

Scared after his immersion in the river Ojuk clings tightly to a helper.

nights in the forest. After only a fortnight of freedom he vanished, and it was 3 weeks before he re-appeared at the feeding place. He did not seem either exhausted or particularly hungry; he just came to be fed as if he had never been away. Above all he seemed to have lost every scrap of interest in us humans. We were very pleased; that, after all, was just as it should be.

Shortly after his return from the forest Pesek received a visit. The Immigration Officer and his family, to whom Pesek had belonged, came with some friends to the station to make sure he was all right. Though we asked them not to touch or feed the orangs, they managed to smuggle two bottles of orangeade and a big bag of biscuits up the path to the feeding place for their former pet. We scarcely dared hope that Pesek would be able to resist these enticements of civilization. But we underestimated him badly. He no sooner saw his visitors than, perhaps recalling the boredom of confinement, he fled to the top of the highest tree and would not come down again. 'Pesek was very sad that we went away without him', the head of the family confided to us later. 'I could see quite clearly the way he was crying. He would so much have liked to have come home with us!' We could only nod our sympathy.

So Pesek had turned into a half-wild orang without too much difficulty; during his 3 weeks absence he had proved to us that he could feed himself. Yet now he was again to be found regularly at the feeding place. Most of our orangs seemed to come back sooner or later, sometimes after long gaps. Often they came with full bellies and faces smeared with fruit juice. They had found in the forest better things to eat than our monotonous banana diet and no longer needed the supplement – yet still they came back. We supposed that it offered them an opportunity for play and other social contact – a kind of community centre, perhaps, with morning and afternoon tea laid on.

From this point onwards we reduced the feed that we gave to

apes on their way to independence. First we excluded them from the morning feed, and then from the afternoon party too. A few orangs took the hint and went their way, coming back months later or not at all. They had taken for themselves the final step back to the wild. About two-thirds of them came back regularly, however, even though there was no food at all for them. Sometimes we would grab them and weigh them, holding them tightly under the arms and stepping onto a scale. An occasional weight check, together with their general appearance, told us whether these animals were really feeding themselves in the forest or not. Like most of the half-wild orangs, Pesek didn't take kindly to being grabbed round the middle and weighed. No longer used to being handled, he found the contact unpleasant and wriggled out of it as soon as possible.

It was 2 months since we had stopped feeding them. Pesek, Pandi and six other orang utans, all released at the same time, were doing fine. Two others who had also had no food were losing weight: at around 4 years they were still on the young side, and we decided to feed them again giving them a few months more to get used to living wild. The eight who had proved themselves capable of living without human support were a bit of a problem: we felt that even their infrequent visits to the station meant that they were not yet entirely free of our influence. So we determined to move them, by helicopter, to another part of the reserve altogether, just as soon as we could. There they would be able to begin their life as wild animals properly in the undisturbed depths of the rain forest, far from Bohorok station and all other human settlements.

11
Orangs by the Dozen

Unhappily for us and our planning, Ibu Alex left Medan. Her husband was posted to Java and she of course went with him. Some of her influence remained, but we had lost both a friend and a powerful ally. We tackled on our own the two senior police officers whose orangs she had told us about, and found that, without Ibu Alex to support us, they were hard indeed to convince. Why should they give up their orangs? They loved them dearly – couldn't bear to be parted – the children would be desolate without them: Regina and I used our best powers of persuasion for several months on end but the two chiefs of police, polite but firm, refused to budge an inch.

So we took a lesson from some old Indonesian wisdom, passed on to us with tongue-in-cheek by Pawang Husin. 'If you want to get something out of the boss,' he chuckled, 'buy his wife a cake.' For Regina and me it was relatively easy to infiltrate the circle in which these upper-class ladies moved socially: they were interested in us and our work, and – just occasionally – we felt we could afford to attend a civilized party away from our work at Bohorok. So at last we met the two wives over coffee. Already they had heard about us from Ibu Alex – and probably from their husbands too. They knew we had designs on their household orangs, and were not in the least dismayed. They knew why we wanted them. Friendly and sympathetic, they promised to talk to their husbands about releasing the animals to us.

With these two, luck was on our side. Both of their husbands were due for posting to Java in a year or so, and they wouldn't be able to take the orangs with them. Worn out by long harassment from us, and perhaps nagged as well by their wives, the two chiefs of police finally decided, almost at the same moment, to give their animals to us instead of handing them over as a present to their successors. So, just before they left for Java, we collected their three orangs, all healthy and well kept, and carried them home in triumph to the quarantine cages.

Securing these three took the best part of a year. With others it was even longer. Perhaps our most difficult customer was Mr Chindri, a wealthy and influential Medan business man, and proud owner of Untung ('lucky'), an almost fully grown female. We met Mr Chindri's wife, a pretty young Chinese, through the wife of one of our chiefs of police. Mrs Chindri took us home and introduced us to Untung, who was sitting sadly, dull and withdrawn, in a garden cage. 'Careful, she bites!' called Mrs Chindri when I walked up to Untung, but the orang took no notice of her or of me: she sat listless, staring into the treetops beyond the garden wall. Like many grown orangs kept long in captivity, she had changed from a merry, playful youngster to a surly adult. Mrs Chindri was clearly afraid of her, and hoped her husband would let us collect her for release.

But Mr Chindri would have none of it. When we drove up to the house to see him a few days later, the servants turned us away. The orang has gone, they said, sent away by the master. It wasn't true: Untung was still in her cage in the garden. But Mr Chindri saw no reason for letting us in – even less for our taking his orang away. Nor would he admit the PPA into his garden; even the police were unable to pass through the tall iron gates that guarded his house.

In the months that followed we tried doggedly to get on speaking terms with the Chindris again. But our efforts were in vain. Then one day, when we had almost forgotten about them, an express letter arrived from our doctor and friend in Medan,

Dr Kosasih. 'Please collect the orang from the Chindris straightaway.' it said. 'She is very aggressive and has eaten nothing for five days.'

Untung was probably eleven years old by then, a mature, fully grown orang. From Dr Kosasih's message I gathered that she was either unmanageable or very ill. In case Mr Chindri changed his mind, I drove the same day to Medan, equipped with a crate and a tranquillizing injection. 'Splendid of you to come so quickly', said Mrs Chindri, obviously relieved beyond measure to see me. Very soon an old servant appeared, leading Untung by the hand. When I had last seen her, Untung had been listless and dispirited; now she was a wretched, miserable wreck. All skin and bone, she wobbled on shaky legs as the servant led her up to us. Her face had collapsed; her skin was wrinkled and her hair matted and dull. 'She won't eat any more,' said Mrs Chindri, 'She must be very sad.' I stepped forward and approached Untung, talking quietly to her. Then I began to stroke her. Sad she certainly was, but she was desperately ill too, from malnutrition and any of half-a-dozen possible diseases. Once again the warning came: '*Awas, gigit*' – 'Careful, she bites!', but nothing was further from Untung's thoughts. She climbed without resisting into my crate, whimpering a little as the lid was shut; but a moment later accepted a juicy young cucumber and held it firmly in her hands.

So in the end, after 3 years of effort, we got this orang too – and only because her owner was frightened of seeing her die. Untung was suffering from chronic amoebic dysentery, and was undernourished, as she probably had been for years. It took months – long after I had left Bohorok – to get her fit and cheerful, but now once again she is free in the forest and lives up to her name – Untung, the lucky one.

Time and patience brought Untung to Bohorok. With Nakal it was guile – some might say out-and-out theft. One bright day in August found Mr Bangun and me driving in a taxi through the middle of the Medan bird market. Our new Toyota with its

WWF insignia was hidden away round a corner. We stopped at a shabby booth. I was a tourist; Mr Bangun in his oldest scruffiest clothes, played the role of interpreter and guide.

'This lady here wants to buy your orang', said Mr Bangun in Indonesian. He was introducing me to a bird seller, who eyed me suspiciously from the front of his booth. Bamboo cages of all sizes and shapes covered the ground around us; there were more swinging over our heads, from bamboo poles stuck in the ground. In the cages were pigeons of every size and colour, alone or in tight-packed groups. There were grackels, too, and a few orioles and shamas, hopping around and singing sad, monotonous little songs. Stray dogs and cats wandered among them, picking up scraps and squabbling over leftovers. We were not really there to buy an orang or anything else. We had heard, in the Hotel Danau Toba, that one of the market traders was holding a baby orang; now we pretended to be visitors who wanted to pick up an orang on the black market.

'I should like to see the animal first,' I said politely in English. Mr Bangun interpreted and the bird seller disappeared into the depths of his shabby blue stall. Almost immediately he was back – on his arm a tiny, scrawny red-haired orang, stiff with dirt and whimpering to himself in the sudden bright light. So far so good. We'd confirmed that there really was an orang, but we had to move carefully. Mr Bangun could not confiscate it without police support, but we knew that trader and orang would disappear without trace into the crowd if we gave the least cause for suspicion. So we kept up the pantomime. I looked over the wretched little animal critically and asked the price. '60,000 rupiah', came the instant reply, and Mr Bangun duly translated for me -- well over £120. Clearly, our drab brown taxi was helping to mark us out as rich foreign tourists, ripe for fleecing.

I started to haggle. 'Much too much', I said. 'It's absolutely tiny and probably sick as well. I'm certainly not going to give more than 10,000 for him!' There was more of this, with Mr

Bangun translating laboriously at every stage. Finally we agreed on 30,000 rupiah – half the original price. Then came the crunch. 'I have no money on me, and its Saturday – so I can't go to the bank. I am sure the hotel manager will cash me a cheque. Why don't you come to the hotel tomorrow morning, and we'll fix the deal then?'

The dealer paused a moment, then suddenly pushed the little animal into my arms, pressing it on me in both senses of the word. 'No, take him with you now, and I'll come for the money in the morning.' He was obviously nervous, and wanted at all costs to avoid moving through the streets with the animal. I glanced questioningly at Mr Bangun, but the bird seller had already disappeared into the back of his stall. So we got into the taxi with the shivering orang and drove off, changing into the Toyota just round the corner and heading for home.

I stopped for a few minutes to buy a bottle and some milk for Nakal ('scamp') as I had named him, so that he wouldn't be hungry on the way. Nakal was still looking pathetic, but the name somehow matched his character, and I hoped might be a good omen for him. On the way back to Bohorok he sat contentedly on my lap, watching the moving scenery and now and then taking a greedy suck at the bottle. Examining him more closely I discovered he must be about 8 months old; he hadn't yet grown all of his milk teeth. There could be no doubt that his mother had been killed, for no orang mother would willingly give up her baby at that age.

The capture had not left Nakal unmarked; one of his eyes was covered with a bluish film, which almost certainly meant partial blindness, and his right arm was swollen and crooked, obviously a badly healed fracture. We could find no external injuries or inflammation and he had no fever, so we decided to leave his limb alone. Nakal used it quite freely, snatching with it at the bottle, and even his blind eye didn't seem to worry him or affect his aim. It was weeks before he recovered his strength and started to grow again.

Back in Medan the bird seller got off lightly. Calling at the hotel next morning for his money, he was met by Mr Bangun – now in his official capacity and uniform – and a policeman. They told him that we had moved on, that the little orang had been confiscated, and that he had no claim to compensation – indeed that he'd better not break the law again. Chalked up as a success for the PPA, this helped to spread word of their increasing vigilance in tracking down and confiscating orangs wherever they could. It was another small nail in the coffin of the illicit trade, and we were glad to have had a hand in driving it home.

Our adventure with Nakal was shortly to be matched by an even more blatant theft – Markus's kidnapping of Riau. Accompanied by his brother Berni (who was staying with us for a brief visit) Markus had been on a rhino survey, exploring the swamp forests of Riau, a central province of Sumatra. Calling in at a remote oil camp, they heard that one of the American prospectors was keeping a young female orang at a house in a nearby village. Markus investigated, and found that the orang – a strikingly beautiful animal with vivid red hair – was intended as a present from the oil company to the Governor of Riau. It was all legal and above-board, said the public-relations man who dealt with his enquiries. In no way, he added, was the animal available for rehabilitation. No sir.

Markus dug further. He discovered that the owner of the orang had already been directed by the PPA to surrender the animal to a rehabilitation station, though the PPA again could not enforce its order. They referred Markus to the Governor who was intended to receive the present. Markus, hoping at least for a hearing, waited unavailingly for 3 days to see the Governor, and waited a fourth day on the promise of an interview with his secretary. Then Swiss patience ran out. Driving back to the village, Berni and the local PPA man beside him, he seized the orang from its keepers (who were glad to see the back of it) and had it crated up for travel. With the animal in the box, and the box tied down in the back of the Toyota, he began the long drive back to Bohorok.

Ten minutes along the road an American car passed him on its way to the village, the driver waving in a friendly way. Markus and Berni waved back, then realized that they had just passed the owner of the orang. Markus stepped on the accelerator and drove without a stop, putting the greatest possible mileage between themselves and a US citizen who would shortly be very angry indeed.

After a day-long drive on abominable roads they stopped at our friends the Janssens for a breather, opening the crate to let Riau – as they decided to call her – out for a breather too. Riau had been used to short walks before. But this time her notion of a breather involved more than a brief walk. The moment the lid of her crate was lifted, she climbed out and darted up the nearest tree – which happened to be a particularly large one. Surrounded as it was by gardens and plantations, this was no place to leave a newly-released orang: Riau had to be caught. In an astonishing feat which combined the skills of climbing and rope-work, Berni shinned up the tree after her, trussed her like a turkey with coils of nylon line, and lowered her gently back into her crate.

I was away from the station when the men returned with Riau. Regina remembers how the crate was opened and the splendid, red animal climbed out, first one arm and then the other reaching up to grasp the bars of the quarantine-cage roof. Riau hung from the ceiling with feet almost touching the ground; the morning sun shone from behind the cage, lighting her hair in a fiery halo round the dark silhouette of her body. Her dramatic rescue and introduction to Bohorok were entirely in keeping with this marvellous animal's character, as we were soon to learn.

Riau made a tremendous impression on all who came into contact with her. Physically and mentally she was overwhelming – an orang super-girl, strong and playful, with a mind very much of her own. From first arrival she dominated – amiably but with determination. When Riau wanted to play, someone had to play with her; if she wanted to walk, no bars would hold her. She exasperated, even intimidated the keepers, and we usually worked in pairs in her cage. Though never belligerent, she teased us, grabbing the brooms when we came to muck her out, grasping our hair and our clothes in handfuls, and rubbing us playfully with strong white teeth.

Our quarantine cages didn't suit her at all. Too small to contain her demonic energy, they were also too weak: she soon learned to force the bars so she could slip out for a gambol whenever she felt like it. Eternally playful, she would bound up to us like a huge, friendly spider when we returned tired from the forest or river track, demanding to be rolled and punched and shaken. It was never difficult to put her back, but the staff grew weary of mending her cage. For Riau, rehabilitation was an irksome formality in an otherwise agreeable life, and we had to change the rules for her. As soon as the mandatory quarantine period was up we let her go free, watching with some relief as she climbed into the forest above the feeding station.

It was wonderful to watch her climb. Every orang utan has its own style of climbing, as individual as a human walk. Despite her months of captivity, Riau climbed fast and elegantly, with arms and legs working in perfect co-ordination. She knew all about building nests, and characteristically ordered her own social arrangements. The second day of her freedom, a young wild male came to the feeding place and began to woo her enthusiastically. During the next 3 or 4 days her interest in humans withered, and after a week she disappeared with her new companion into the depths of the Reserve. A few days later we saw her again, sitting with her boyfriend high up above us. Positive as always, she was smacking her lips in threat and throwing branches down. Feeling like unwanted gooseberries, we crept humbly away.

It was some months since our first highly productive visit to

Aceh and the west coast, and time to make contact again with
Gersom Sinaga, the PPA representative in Kandang. Gersom,
we knew, already had another confiscated orang waiting to be
collected. Regina planned a journey that would take her up
north and round to Kandang, arranging to give a lecture and
slide show in Banda Aceh on the way. In August 1974 Elisabeth
and Alex, two friends of hers, come out to visit us from Switzerland. Elisabeth and Alex – both doctors – wanted to see as much
of Sumatra as possible; Regina wanted to visit the north and
west. It made good sense for them to combine forces and make
the journey together. In a Toyota loaned by the PPA and driven
by a lively young nephew of Mr Bangun's, they started out early
one morning in August. The driver, it turned out, had much to
learn of the finer points of driving. In the first few miles he
scared his passengers to death, knocked over an old lady –
fortunately without hurting her – and earned the nickname
'Fittipaldi'. He was relieved of his duties on all but the straight-
est, safest and least-inhabited roads.

Regina and her party passed through Medan, Binjai and
Lhok Seumawe, reaching Banda Aceh on the second day. They
watched the rice being harvested from enormous paddy fields
that stretched to the horizon, and saw water-buffaloes patiently
plodding round and round on the threshing floors. At Banda
Aceh Regina delivered her slide show under the auspices of the
local PPA; it went down well, stirring up local interest in our
work at Bohorok. Then they continued along the rough, rocky
west coast road, through the fishing villages, across the sandy
beaches and over the headlands that had so intrigued us the year
before. Crossing the streams on plank bridges and the rivers on
cable ferries, they passed through the villages of Meulaboh and
Blangpidie, and Tapaktuan, a small town, where they stopped
for food and a rest. At each stop Regina made a point of talking
to the local people about captive orangs, sometimes eliciting a
promise from the local headman or policeman that one or two
would be waiting for them when they returned in a few days'

time. Finally they reached Kandang, where Gersom Sinaga and his wife welcomed them warmly.

The party travelled on south to pay a brief visit to the Kluet reserve, falling for its magic just as we had done. Then began the long journey back. At Kandang, where they stayed the night, they collected their first orang, a 3-year-old female called Sumbing, whom Gersom had confiscated from a timber camp some weeks before. Sumbing (the name means hare-lip) had a split lower lip, a deformity that may well have reduced her value and saved her from being sold illicitly for export to some miserable oriental zoo. She was a sorry-looking creature, undernourished and dishevelled, but she made no fuss when they crated her for the journey to Bohorok, and travelled stoically over the rough road in the back of the Toyota.

At Tapaktuan the first overnight stop, they got to know Sumbing better. In the hotel bedroom they gave her a meal of condensed milk and bananas, which she ate with gusto. She had some difficulty in drinking, using her tongue to stop the milk running away through her cleft lip. Regina and her medically-minded friends wondered how she had managed to suckle as a baby, a problem often experienced by human infants with the hare-lip deformity. Sumbing turned out to be very gentle and well-mannered. Though by far the ugliest orang we had acquired, she stole our hearts by her sheer charm. She was not at all demanding – just happy to sit beside someone with her hand on their arm. She specially loved having the back of her neck rubbed; if you stopped, she would gently take your hand and put it back, asking you to continue. That night they didn't even return her to her box. She slept on a sack beside Regina's bed, creeping up onto the bed in the small hours and sleeping until daybreak at Regina's side.

Next morning the party stopped at Blangpidie, where the local policeman was already sitting in front of the hotel when they drew up, and took them 8 to 10 kilometres out to another settlement where the orang was kept. Here the policeman and Regina worked the ruse that Mr Bangun and I had pulled in the bird market at Medan. Regina became a potential buyer, and the men of the village hurried off to produce their captive orang for her inspection. The orang turned out to be a dark adolescent male about 10 years old, crouching in the corner of a sapling cage. Regina looked it over and asked the men to put it in the back of the Toyota. Rather to her surprise they did so without demur. Just as she and the policeman were preparing to unmask themselves, fate took a hand in the drama; the bottom of the cage fell out, and the orang – very sensibly, in the circumstances – wasted no time in climbing the nearest tree.

Quick action by Alex saved the situation. With a leap that surprised everyone he grabbed one of the disappearing animal's legs and hung on grimly. The rest of them shook the tree, and Alex slowly gained advantage; arm by arm the surprised orang let go and fell to the ground, where everyone pounced on him. Elisabeth and Regina gave him a tranquillizing injection in the thigh, and he relaxed philosophically. They soon had him safely stowed in a travelling crate, but still had to settle accounts with the villagers.

None of the men said a word. Regina was not sure whether it was a hostile silence, or whether the villagers were simply speechless after the recapture. Not waiting to enquire, she gave them a letter from Gersom Sinaga explaining who she was and why she was authorized to collect orangs on behalf of the PPA. The letter pointed out the iniquities of those who caught and traded in orangs, and the law's view of the matter – which of course the villagers knew perfectly well. Then Regina gave the policeman his bus fare back to Blangpidie, and the villagers went their separate ways. Regina could not blame the villagers for capturing and trying to sell an orang; they were poor people who needed every penny they could scrape together. The guilty ones – and I shared her views in this – were those who continued to flout the law by offering good prices for orangs, and thus made illicit dealing worth while.

Regina and her party picked up two more young males at Kuala Simpang. The first, a lively youngster from a private collection, was rounded up and boxed without difficulty. The second, collected by foresters from a timber-felling concession, was a shy animal about 4 years old, obviously taken recently from the wild. It had spent the previous few days in a cage in the Forestry Office garden, but was unresponsive when Regina approached and talked kindly to it. The head forester was a little reluctant to hand his charge over to this strange, rather scruffy party of travellers whose credentials were none too obvious. But in conversation Regina discovered that he was a worried man. His wife, who had recently had a baby, was lying at home with a high fever, and there was no local doctor for miles around. Elisabeth and Alex were able to introduce themselves as doctors. They examined the forester's wife and discussed a course of treatment with the district nurse, to everyone's immense relief. This set the forester's mind at rest. If he had had a dozen orangs to dispose of, he would happily have given them all to Regina and her friends after that.

Getting this recently captured young ape into a travelling crate was a tricky problem. Still wild and unused to handling, he hung on hard to the grille of his cage and bared his teeth menacingly at anyone who came within reach. A crowd of people gathered to see the fun, and their laughter and shouts alarmed him still more. On top of this it was late evening, and getting too dark to see properly. This time Alex solved the problem by driving the Toyota in front of the cage and shining the headlights on the scene. Regina bravely entered the cage and grabbed the orang under the arms; at the same time the others prized his hands and feet off the grille and he was bundled, still protesting, into the crate.

The travellers returned exhausted to Bohorok, and I helped them to unload their cargo of orangs. Sumbing immediately established herself as favourite with us all. Her appetite was insatiable, as if she had years on short rations to make up for. She put on weight well, seeming to grow broader rather than taller; as time went on she developed a fine paunch which with her bright eyes and spindly limbs made her look like a cheerful, intelligent spider. She was never a problem; once released, she soon became independent and wandered off for days at a stretch on her own.

The dark adolescent from Blangpidie we called Momok, meaning 'spook' or 'bogey-man'; he looked like a phantom from the forest. But he was sweet-natured and curiously shy. For a long time he would eat only when he was on his own; the moment he saw anyone coming, he would climb onto his shelf and hide his face in the corner of the cage. He had an entertaining trick, too, which none of the others shared, of hanging his empty banana skins in orderly rows along the bottom bar of his cage. In fact, Momok turned out to have several strong ideas of his own, and they didn't include staying caged up for long. As soon as he was over his innoculations he managed to escape as his cage was being cleaned, and disappeared like a phantom through the tree-tops. It was some months before we saw him again – in a durian plantation some distance from Bohorok where we were called in to catch three robber-orangs. Momok, the ringleader, we identified first from his colour, then from a distinctive broken toe which we had noted as a minor injury on his record card.

The stroppy young orang from the private collection in Kuala Simpang we named after his home village. Simpang took some time to get over the ordeal of his former captivity, but eventually turned into a handsome adolescent and went his way. Our fourth acquisition, the wild young male from the forester's garden, never settled at all in captivity. We liberated him with some relief the moment his quarantine was over. We called him Goyang ('shaker') because he constantly threatened us by shaking branches at us. He disappeared shortly after release and we never saw him again.

Keen as we were to take in orangs, there were times when we had to think twice about accepting one – or at least look closely into the circumstances of its capture. We had vowed, early on, never to buy one or give a reward directly for an orang; that would merely have encouraged people to continue trading illicitly. But we could occasionally pay out-of-pocket expenses to someone who had genuinely helped us, and even pay contacts who went out of their way to find orangs in captivity for us. One such contact was Chang. A Chinese from Kuala Simpang, Chang was a professional police informer, hunting chiefly for illegal marijuana plantations in the back country. His work took him to the remotest corners of the northern area, and we paid him a small retainer each month to keep us informed about any captive orangs that he heard about in his travels.

One day while I was away from the station, Chang called in and saw Regina. After greeting her in his rather oily way, he told her that he had confiscated a young female orang on a plantation near Kuala Simpang. He promised to send it, and asked her to make good his expenses – of which he produced a formidable list from his pocket. This was contrary to our agreement with Chang, for we had never promised to pay expenses other than those involved in moving an animal. Regina was suffering from fever at the time and not really at her best. But she was alert enough to smell a rat. She paid Chang, but remained highly suspicious of his story. Her suspicions deepened when the orang was delivered a few days later. 'Susila' (the name means 'respectable') was certainly no more than 3 years old; thin as a rake, with patchy coat, she was very shy and seemed not to have been long in captivity. To Regina she looked more like a recent capture than a long-standing plantation pet. Chang had disappeared, so Regina determined to visit Kuala Simpang as soon as possible and get to the bottom of the mystery.

As luck had it, some of our Chinese friends in Medan had relations in Kuala Simpang, so Regina's task was made easier. She took with her on the journey an elderly Chinese lady – the mother of our Medan friends – who knew many of the Chinese community in Kuala Simpang. A former school teacher, the lady had left Shanghai as a young girl over half a century before.

She passed the time on the long journey by telling Regina one fascinating story after another about her life in old China and the former East Indies. At the end of their journey, long after dark, Regina spent the night with the old lady's family. On the following morning, from the son of the house, she heard the full, sad story of Susila's capture.

The son, it turned out, was the owner of the plantation where Susila was taken. Susila and her mother had lived in a remnant of forest close to the plantation. They were well known to everyone, and the little damage they did was tolerated. But then Chang came along and saw a chance of profit. He promised some of the villagers a motor-cycle if they caught the young orang alive for him. So they trapped the two orangs on the ground, clubbing the mother to death and capturing Susila. Chang took Susila and may have tried to sell her locally, but failed. As her condition deteriorated he thought of Bohorok, and cut his losses by passing her off to us with an inflated expense sheet.

We reported Chang's dishonesty to the PPA and the police, who started an investigation. But when they asked for witnesses, nobody would come forward. Too many of the villagers were involved, and even the body of the mother could no longer be found. So Chang got away with it – or almost so. We didn't employ him any more, and the villagers – whose motor-cycle never materialized – probably gave him a hard time when next he was down their way. We were not happy about the result. Was paying an informer a good way of going about things? Were we part-responsible for his dishonesty? Chang was a poor man with a big family, and their welfare was probably more important to him than any number of orangs. Could we really blame him – or any other poor Indonesian who tried to augment his income by catching and selling an orang? We laid the blame squarely on the shoulders of the foreigners and well-to-do Indonesians whose money and influence kept the black market alive.

12
Visitors and Doctors

As the weeks and months passed we settled firmly into our little station. More than just a research centre, it became our home, where we lived simply but comfortably and developed a pleasant routine of work. We started early in the morning and had usually done most of the active jobs before the full heat of the day. The tea party in the late afternoon rounded off the day's work outside. Then one of us would go back down the hill to make supper, while the other watched till dark to see all the free orangs safely to their nests. Returning after dark to our little house-on-stilts, we were always delighted to walk slowly up the last few metres of the path, with the soft light of the Tilly-lamp welcoming us across the verandah. Wumi was usually there to greet us with a friendly bark and vigorously wagging tail. The smell of supper, wafting through the open windows, told us it was time to relax and enjoy the evening.

The kitchen was the place where, almost every evening, we talked over the problems of the day and set the world to rights. Visitors may have seen it as a dreary, functional sort of place, but we loved it. Opposite the entrance from the verandah was a big window with round wooden bars to keep out unwelcome intruders. In front stood a big kitchen table with the kerosene cooker on top. The window looked out onto the luxuriant green of banana trees behind the house. Unfortunately the little wild bananas were inedible, even when ripe, so we left them to the cockroaches that swarmed in the trees.

On the left of the window was the wall with the bathroom door and water tank in the corner. We once toyed with the thought of keeping goldfish in the bathroom water tank. But water from it could flow into the kitchen water tank, and the idea of drinking goldfish-water tea didn't appeal to either of us. On the wooden wall above the tank hung various sizes of saucepans with their lids, and other cooking utensils crowded beside them. On the remaining two walls were racks and shelves for our food. What was on those depended on when we had last been shopping in the village or Medan.

Just to the right of the entrance from the verandah stood the kerosene refrigerator, the most costly item in the whole kitchen. Sometimes it worked and sometimes it didn't, but we gradually got used to its ways; it kept us in cool drinks for much of the time, and we often stored blood samples and other biological specimens in it, for the kitchen doubled as a laboratory. Beyond lay the two bedrooms, and between them the terrace which was also our sitting room and study. With all the windows and doors open there was usually a gentle breeze through the house, enough to keep us cool and refreshed most evenings.

Apart from Regina, Wumi and me, all sorts of other creatures lived in our house from time to time. Not all of them were ideal companions. For instance we had a colony of ants that lived under the step. They were entirely nocturnal; we didn't see them at all during the day so we tended to forget they were there. If we went out of the house in the evening with bare feet they leapt out and bit us hard. The termites were not much fun either. They used to trek one behind the other in endless processions up one of the pillars outside the house, across the wall to my bedroom window. They trekked along the window frame to a place where there was a tiny hole in the mosquito netting; I often wonder how they ever came to find it. Through the netting and into the room, they promenaded along the wall to the bookshelf, and along the bookshelf to my files and notebooks, into which they disappeared. Shaking them off, smoking them out, even spraying with insecticide did no good at all. There were too many of them with the same idea. Quiet, methodical and persistent, in the end they won. Working diagonally through my carefully collected scientific literature, they ate passages and caves to provide nurseries for their young. Notepaper too was a special treat for them, the more expensive the better. Fortunately they didn't like books, and we were thankful that they left the fabric of the house and our clothes alone.

But our worst lodgers by far were the cockroaches. Up to 2 inches long, they swarmed all over the house and found their way into every cranny. We sprayed and fumigated to keep them down, but there was little point; the forest outside was full of them too. For every one we killed indoors, a dozen more were waiting to move in. The crevices between the floor and wall-boards were just the right size for them and made ideal hide-outs. As soon as it got dark, they started pushing their long antennae out; the moment we doused the lights they emerged to scuttle and fly across the room in every direction. I hated using a torch when I had to get up at night, because it lit up the dozens of cockroaches sitting all over the bedside table and the walls. We caught them in traps – tall glasses with syrup in the bottom; we swatted and stamped on them. But they were always with us.

One night I had a dream. I was playing with a little mouse, that suddenly grew tired of the game and bit my finger. I woke up immediately to find my finger smarting, as though I really had been bitten; in fact it was bleeding – the skin had been nipped. The next night I woke up again with a sharp pain in one of my fingers, and felt something move away from my hand with a dry, rustling sound. I lit the lamp; once again there was a piece of skin missing, and this time I found the culprit – a large, smug-looking cockroach, waving his antennae at me from the bedside table. For a long time after that I always spent a good hour hunting cockroaches all over my room before going to bed.

We had nicer lodgers too. Walman, a fat green skink – a sort of bow-legged lizard – sometimes came and sat on our work table around midday, picking flies and moths off the fly-screens. A delightful little toad with golden eyes used to spend the day sleeping on the edge of the water tank in our bathroom. In the evening he took off down the drain, finding his way back again as the day dawned. Now and then a big monitor lizard would take a stroll around the house to see if we had put out any scraps of meat for him. He particularly liked chicken heads and feet, but scavenged quite impartially. Then he usually took a little rest in the shade of the house before plodding down to the river, to slide elegantly into the water and vanish from sight.

People brought us animals too. Apart from the orangs we received a succession of owls, macaques, gibbons and simians, a young leopard that Wumi raised, a civet cat and even a slow loris, which we liberated as soon as we could. We had no intention of keeping household pets other than Wumi, and gibbons, tree-snakes and giant spiders were so plentiful outside the house that we saw no point in bringing them in. As zoologists we revelled in the dozens of different kinds of animals that came to visit us, and only wished we had time to give them more of our attention.

Human visitors came too to stay at Bohorok. We tried to make them all welcome, though our accommodation was very strictly limited. There were times when we had to point out that we were there to do a job, and were not running a tourist camp for casual holiday-makers. The nicest guests helped with the work, paid their way, enjoyed the forest, the orangs, the birds and all the other marvellous things to be seen around the centre, and moved on before they outstayed their welcome. The others loafed, told us their troubles, got in the way and tried to distract us from what we were doing. We were especially pleased when old friends from Europe came out to visit us. Then we could settle around the table in the evening and talk nostalgically of all that was happening back home.

Among our stranger visitors was an American lawyer and naturalist, who wanted to discover whether orangs, like men, could put on an act and lie. With wild black hair and a beard to match, he was a striking addition to our little community, especially when he stood on his head on the verandah as part of his spiritual exercises. This puzzled Wumi, who always barked and tried to lick his face when she found him upside down. Another visitor, far more rational in every way, was Robert Olivier, an Englishman working on South-east Asian elephants. Robert was a dedicated naturalist and excellent company. He helped with the work of the station, and took full advantage of his stay with us. On expeditions into the forest with Regina and Markus he was rewarded with the never-to-be-forgotten sight of a herd – no fewer than seven – of the very rare elephants he had come to study.

We had many photographers, including two out-and-out professionals – Dieter Plage and Mike Price of Anglia Television – who make the world famous 'World of Survival' series. The producer, Colin Willock, and his wife also joined us for a short time. Survival made a one-hour television film we were all proud of called 'Orang Utan, Orphans of the Forest'. There were other cameramen too. I remember especially a huge bear of a man from Singapore whose enthusiasm knew no bounds. He started filming on the path from Bukit Lawang, and was engrossed with filming the river crossing when the overburdened canoe sank under him. None of his expensive equipment was lost, but he had to spend many hours taking cameras and meters to pieces and drying them out over the stove. Shooting close-ups of the orangs at the feeding station, he was unwise enough to leave one of his more elaborate cameras unattended by the cages. Doli, who had been watching him attentively, swooped down and stole it. Leaping up to the tree tops with the camera dangling nonchalantly from her free hand, she examined it closely. Then she let it drop. Fortunately for the cameraman it fell into a bush and remained in one piece.

We even had a scout from a tourist organization, seeking locations for adventure holidays off the beaten track. He too fell foul of the river; one afternoon we had to haul him out with the washing-line when the current proved too strong. But he enjoyed Bohorok and went home fully determined to include us in one of his tour itineraries. Occasionally there were parties of visitors we couldn't explain at all – a pair of Russian-speaking sisters from Tokyo, for example, who turned up in the company of an Australian zoo-keeper and an American co-ed studying psychology. How they had met, and what brought them jointly to Bohorok, we never managed to fathom.

Among our most memorable and useful visitors were Alex and Elisabeth, the two Swiss doctor friends of Regina's, who came out to spend a few weeks with us in July and August 1974. After their journey with Regina to the west coast, they stayed and helped us about the station. We were lucky to have them with us just at that time, for one of the orangs needed skilled medical attention which they were able to supply.

Their patient was Comel, a 5-year-old male who had recently come to us from the PPA. In good condition, he had passed quickly and uneventfully through rehabilitation to freedom, and was now a frequent visitor to the tea-parties. Comel turned up one day at the feeding place with a fresh wound at the back of his ankle, so we brought him down to the quarantine cage near the house, where we could keep an eye on him. At first we thought the injury was small and would heal quickly, but then we saw that he could not move his foot at all. That meant that the exterior muscle or its tendon had been damaged – possibly a crippling condition for an animal that spent most of its time climbing trees.

Comel's injury reminded us uneasily that, during the past few weeks, several apes had returned to the feeding with cuts and other injuries. Most of them were minor – hardly worth bothering about – but one or two were serious; we had even taken some of the affected animals into Medan for treatment by one of our doctor friends. Some of the caged animals had developed slight injuries too. We had searched the whole area around the cages for protruding nails and sharp edges, but in spite of everything the injuries continued. It was puzzling because, caged or in the wild, orangs seldom did things that might result in injury. We had often noticed how careful and clever they were with dangerous objects like nails, splinters of glass and knives. Were there other animals involved – siamangs, perhaps (we'd sometimes seen them attacking orangs in the tree-tops), or even bears or tigers? But most of the injuries, like Comel's, were more like clean cuts than bites.

Elisabeth and Alex examined Comel and left us in no doubt; his cut heel looked like a knife wound. If other orangs were injured in similar ways, then someone who could get close to them was slashing them with a knife – just enough to inflict small but noticeable cuts. It was a nasty thought. We put all-night guards on the cages and kept a special look-out for strangers, and we racked our brains to think of anyone who might bear us or the orangs this particular kind of grudge. Meanwhile, there was poor Comel to be dealt with.

The wound, already several days old, was not one to be treated easily. Alex and Elisabeth examined it carefully and explained the problem. A severed tendon draws back a long way and becomes difficult to locate, especially with the primitive instruments – little more than one curved needle, some scalpels and battle-worn forceps – that we could muster at the station. But they bravely decided to have a go. We took precise measurements of Comel's foot and made a splint that would allow it to be immobilized at the correct angle. The instruments were sterilized, the kitchen table and Regina's bedside table were scrubbed and covered with clean cloths, and my bedside table was pressed into service as an instrument bench.

Sitting on my lap, Comel himself watched these preparations with great interest. He made no protest when his ankle was lathered with shaving soap, and the hair around the lesion was carefully shaved off. He rather liked the taste of the soap, and wanted to try his hand with the razor. Then he was given a general anaesthetic and quickly went under. While the doctors were scrubbing up we held his leg up in the air, draining the blood vessels by vigorous downward massage and then binding it tightly from the foot toward the knee with crepe bandage. Now Comel was laid on his stomach on the improvised operating table, with cushions under his leg to bring his foot into the right position. A teacloth with a hole in it, specially embroidered by Elisabeth the night before, was laid over the foot so that only the site of the wound showed. With the cloth tied in position round the ankle, we were ready to start.

It was a strange scene – an operating theatre in the middle of the Sumatran rain forest, with two Swiss surgeons in makeshift gear practising their skills on a prostrate ape. By now it was almost midday. Bending over the table, the two doctors already had drops of sweat on their foreheads. With the edges of the wound freshly opened up, they soon saw that the tendon was intact – only the muscle had suffered damage. This made the job easier and the chances of success higher. Sewing up the muscle with thick thread was a tedious business. Alex let fly a robust Swiss oath as a yellow butterfly fluttered over the table and settled on his hand, and we constantly wiped the brows of both surgeons as sweat poured from them.

As they were stitching through the tough skin the worst happened – the only curved needle broke. Luckily the muscle was finished, and it was comparatively easy to complete the job with an ordinary sewing needle. Now and then we bent over to check Comel's pulse and breathing rate, but he was doing well. Then the final stitch was tied, the wound was dressed, and we carefully positioned the splint, binding it into place with bandages. When it was all over we carried Comel – still fast asleep –

into the house and tied him down to a bamboo stretcher especially made for the purpose. It was a good 2 hours later that he started to come round. By evening he was wide awake, though still slightly groggy. He stayed quiet, and we left him alone for the night on the terrace.

We visited him at first light to see how he had slept. Comel had been busy. The stretcher was empty, and the patient greeted us with soft squeaks from the depths of the linen basket. He sat there in state, fully recovered and looking immensely proud of himself. His dressings were scattered across the floor. The splint we had positioned so carefully was in the corner, and already he had taken out every stitch from his skin. Luckily he had not yet got around to the important ones holding the muscle together. There was little we could do about him. Fully recovered from his ordeal, and probably refreshed by his long sleep, he was in no mood to play hospitals. We couldn't get him back on the stretcher or even re-dress his wound. So we gave him a handful of bananas and locked him in a quarantine cage. We washed the wound regularly – there was little else we could do. Fortunately for Comel it healed perfectly. In a few days he could rest on his foot, and in 3 or 4 weeks he was climbing happily in the trees once again. The only tangible evidence of his operation was the teacloth with a neatly embroidered hole, which we treasured for a long time.

Comel was not the last orang to be attacked, and we never really solved the problem of who could be responsible. Strong suspicion fell upon an elderly man who had worked for us briefly and been sacked for dishonesty. Some of the villagers mentioned that he had threatened us when he left, but it was all very vague – certainly not enough to base a prosecution on. There were a few more cuts to be treated during the next two years, but no more after we had moved the feeding site to a slightly different area.

Alex and Elisabeth left shortly after Comel's operation, and we could never again claim a resident medical team at Bohorok.

But several other doctors were associated with our work at different times, and all of them earned our gratitude for their skill and patience. Through the interest of a US medical researcher associated with the US Embassy, we were able to send faecal samples to Jakarta to be checked for parasites and pathogenic bacteria. And the resident doctors in several hospitals of northern Sumatra were kind enough to examine orangs that we had recently acquired, checking their health before we took them to Bohorok. Dr Nurwani Mako Salim, a gifted Indonesian doctor, saved the lives and reduced the sufferings of several of our orangs by her quick and effective diagnoses. Dr Diehl, the senior medical officer of the Goodyear plantation hospital in Dolok Merangir, put his well-equipped surgery at our disposal and made many of our orangs whole after minor accidents.

It was Dr Diehl who helped us when Olip fell out of a tree and broke his jaw. Olip by this time had reached the stage of complete freedom, though he was usually present with a healthy appetite at tea time. When he failed to turn up one morning, Regina assumed that he had wandered off into the freedom of the forest, and would return in the afternoon.

He didn't, and Regina – helped by Purba – found him lying on the ground some distance from the station with his lower jaw smashed. The jaw was already infected – he must have been lying there semi-conscious for several hours. It was a miracle that no predator had found him.

Regina carried Olip back to the station and I drove him to the Goodyear Hospital, 100 km from Medan. I don't suppose Dr Diehl had ever before faced a young orang with a broken jaw, but he knew just what to do. Calm under sedation, Olip was examined and X-rayed, and his jaw was pinned and supported with clips. Six weeks later he returned to the hospital to have his clips removed. Dr. Diehl was impressed; never, he said, had a patient given him less trouble. He'd happily deal with orangs any day.

13
Communication and Behaviour

Some of my best hours at Bohorok were spent just in watching – watching and trying to understand the orangs whose lives were now so inextricably mixed up with my own. I had always been interested in animal behaviour, and to have this group of free, semi-wild animals close and easily observable was a chance that might never come my way again. A good vantage point was the roof of the rehabilitation cages, where I could prop myself comfortably and be still – almost a part of the scenery. A good time for watching was the late afternoon, when the orangs were gathering for the tea-party. There was always plenty of action when half a dozen of them came swinging in from the forest, and my notebooks filled quickly with information and ideas.

It was not only the orangs I watched. The presence of other animals, especially monkeys, often helped me to see how different and special was the behaviour of the orangs. Crab-eating macaques, for example, often came through the forest in troops. They leapt from branch to branch, squabbling and chasing each other through the tree-tops with excited calls, racing up and down the tree-trunks, squeaking, threatening, posturing – in constant noisy communication with each other. It struck me that bustle and noise is typical of most species of primates, man included. By contrast orang utans are curiously quiet. They move slowly and silently, and their vocabulary is limited to a very few sounds, most of them soft and intimate. As loners, orangs seldom meet each other face to face, so it must be especially important that they communicate effectively when they do.

As I sat on the cage roof at feeding time and watched the orangs arriving from all directions, I became especially interested in discovering how they communicated with each other in their close encounters. However human their facial expressions may seem, the sounds they make are strange and unhuman, difficult for us to reproduce and unlinked to our own sounds. This is partly due to their sound-making apparatus, which is quite different from ours. They have a large laryngeal air sac that works like bellows, forcing air through the larynx and acting as a resonance chamber. With it orangs make long-drawn-out rumbles and hoots that we find hard to match. Their sounds are seldom loud, but they carry surprising distances through the forest.

Many of their feelings are communicated by gestures and facial expressions. One day a group of visitors was standing in a group 25 to 30 metres from the cage, while I sat at the feeding place among the orangs. Above me hung Gamat, one of our early acquisitions from the west coast. With both hands clutching a branch, she had one foot idly dangling and the other gripping a strut between the tree and the cage. Gamat turned toward the visitors, making snorting and whistling noises with each breath; the hair on her arms and shoulders was standing on end, making her look larger than life, and she fixed the group with a hard, none-too-friendly stare. Meanwhile, a few branches further back, the fat young male Juluk swung noisily round and round in the foliage, stretching his arms to make himself bigger, and from time to time shaking one of the branches violently. He had thrust his lips forward like a snout, and both he and Gamat snorted and smacked their lips in the direction of the visitors. I wondered if the tourists had any idea

that this was a hostile reaction directed against them. Gamat
and Juluk were saying, in effect, 'We don't know who you are,
and you are too close to our feeding place for us to trust you, so
go away.' I knew the message simply because I had seen it
delivered a dozen times in other circumstances. To other orangs
its meaning would have been unmistakable. The tourists probably thought it was a couple of apes getting excited because it
was nearly banana-time.

As soon as Dekking appeared and emptied his sackful of
bananas onto the roof, Gamat and Juluk forgot their threats and
got down to the serious business of eating. Several other orangs
had already gathered on the roof, and were either sitting
patiently or circling restlessly around Dekking. Almost before
the sack was empty, each had grabbed a handful or two of
bananas, stuck a few more in his mouth and moved slightly
apart to eat in peace. Some, like Pesek, had set up stores of
bananas between their legs and were crouching over them,
smacking their lips in enjoyment of the feast.

Gamat and Juluk came up from the back of the feeding place,
gazing uncertainly at big Pesek and making soft, high-pitched
'ugh-ugh-ugh' sounds. Brief and questioning, these were probably intended to appease Pesek, saying in effect 'We see you are
there and we want to come past, but we wouldn't dream of
touching your bananas.' Pesek said 'Ugh' ('Come on then, but
I'm watching you'), glancing up but continuing his meal. In all
three sounds were made during a quick exhalation with the
mouth closed; I could just hear them 3 or 4 metres away, but
none of the other orangs indicated awareness of their little
conversation.

Gamat and Juluk hurried past Pesek to where Dekking was
holding out rations for them. Then they sat with the rest,
tucking in to their bananas with gusto. Orangs peel bananas
with their lips, either whole or in large pieces, then suck or
chew out the pulp. Sometimes they push their whole lower lip
forward, full of half-chewed banana, and squint at it past their

flat noses. When they have eaten the pulp they sometimes go back to the skins again, gnawing out the white fibres with their incisors.

Now they had all taken the edge off their appetites and some were due for a second course. This is where the fireworks began, because the second course was milk and they were all very fond of it. Dekking lifted a bucket of reconstituted powdered milk onto the cage top and offered a food-can of it to the first of the deserving ones. These were the small, thin orangs, who for one reason or another needed feeding up. But they all crowded around, thin or fat, small or big, in the hopes of getting a few drops or splashes. While the first customer drank from the can, everyone else sat watching anxiously, or pushed their way through the group to where Dekking was squatting. As the second and third drew their rations, lower lips and paws were extended, like spoons to catch any precious drops that might be spilled. They sucked drops from each others' fur, and tried to get one or two fingers into the can, to be licked with relish.

Ucok, a big five-year-old, found a particularly successful way of stealing milk. He would catch little orangs just as they turned away from having their drink, and give them a hearty mouth-to-mouth kiss. The little ones had usually drunk quickly and would still have a big mouthful of milk. Ucok's kiss squeezed some of it out of them and into him.

Waiting for milk that never came was sometimes too much for the youngsters who were no longer given a ration. Sometimes they threw a tantrum, just like a child's tantrum, hammering their head with their fists, screaming shrilly and rolling on the ground in a mixture of rage and desperation. They stopped as quickly as they started. Olip was one who threw tantrums in this way, shrieking and beating his fists on the floor in a fit of instant rage. His friend Purba would often intervene in a kindly, concerned way, but Olip usually recovered and was back to normal in a matter of seconds anyway. Other orangs showed their frustration in different ways. Pakam, for example,

143

shook her hands violently in front of her in an unmistakable gesture – '. . . if only I could get my hands on it . . .' But it never seemed to occur to any of them to chase each other away, or to take by force what they failed to take peacefully by pleas or by cunning.

When most of them had taken all the bananas and milk they could hold, they would often indulge in short sessions of play. Though orangs are usually solitary, they are certainly not anti-social. In the wild, play between adults or even youngsters is probably rare, but mothers play often with their children, and the young ones may play when they and their mothers meet in the tree-tops. The station orangs nearly always took the opportunity to play for a while, sometimes for an hour or so, between the end of the tea-party and nightfall. Social play consisted mainly of wrestling, a sport in which the four hands could be used simultaneously. Wrestling matches often began in the trees, the two contestants hanging by the feet and wrestling with their arms. Or one might wrestle with another on a branch below, tumbling and pulling each other to the ground. Sometimes they would sit together on top of the cages, falling into each others' arms with heads banging together, and ending in a free-for-all with arms and legs entangled.

Olip and Purba had their own style of wrestling. Each clutched the other's coat in a firm grip and nibbled each other; the object seemed to be to nibble at the other's hand or foot while keeping your own four paws safely out of the way. Olip would chew enthusiastically – though obviously painlessly – at Purba's toes, while Purba squeaked with pleasure, mouth open, tongue out and face wrinkled with laughter. In a moment their roles would be reversed. Play-biting was always slow and deliberate. Real bites were sudden and spur-of-the-moment, often an expression of excitement by a nervous or frightened animal. We always moved slowly and quietly to avoid exciting animals that were shy and had not yet got to know us.

Sometimes during the play-hour, as evening drew on, we

Overleaf: Monica watching over the tea party. *Above:* Alan and Elizabeth prepare to operate while Regina holds a foot in position. *Opposite:* Monica with a very young orang clinging to her.

Above: Monica at the tea party. *Opposite:* One Orang drinks from his tin mug while the other looks on with envy.

After the party. Monica, Regina and their assistant play with the young orangs on top of the cages.

Above: The assistant distributes the milk. *Overleaf:* Preparing for freedom.

heard the distant, muffled roar of a lone male, calling some distance away in the tree-tops. It was a strange, eerie sound, almost like the roar of a big cat – a series of throbbing hoots dying away to a soft, intense growl. On hearing it some of the orangs would stop their play for a moment and fall quiet. This was the 'long call' of the local orang-boss, the dominant male who owned the territory in which the station was built. We seldom saw him – he was often away on his travels in other parts of the forest, returning to our area as the fruit ripened, or perhaps as the mood took him. The young males that had stopped at his call continued with their play as soon as he had finished.

We do not know for sure what the long call means. Only fully mature males make it, and John MacKinnon assumes that they use it to notify others that they hold a territory. Neighbouring males know the caller, recognizing him by his voice, and also know whether he is inferior or dominant to them. They can then announce their own presence with a similar long call, or alternatively move on to take up territory elsewhere. The same long call could serve to attract females that are ready for mating.

But the long call, effective over a great distance, is something of an exception in the orang utans' system of communications. Most of their signals are effective only at close quarters, for use when they meet. The low, soft calls and facial expressions, as well as the body postures, seem to be particularly important. In dealing with orangs I realized that I was using 'body-language' or mime myself, to enforce what I said to them. When I shouted in anger I would shake a stick threateningly, or move toward them fast and aggressively; when I spoke to them gently I would stretch out a hand toward them – a friendly and appeasing gesture. I suppose they understood the mime, rather than the words, in the first instance.

We probably used body-language more consciously in earlier stages of our own evolution. That we can still use it becomes apparent when you watch people in conversation, especially if they are excited; deaf mute people especially read the facial expressions and body postures, and see easily if someone is afraid, nervous or embarrassed.

After the play-hour it was time for the orangs to go to bed – or rather, to go off into the forest and build themselves nests for the night. Some of them, especially those that had been long in captivity, were still not very good at this. Others were too full of food and too comfortable to exert themselves. These we had to chase up into the trees, so they would get the habit – perhaps re-establish a lost habit – of building themselves an overnight roost well away from the ground. Here, too, body language was important, and so was the authority that Dekking possessed over them. Some of the young males especially had little respect for Regina or me. There was hardly any doubt that they under-stood us when we told them to get up into the trees, but they didn't always feel inclined to do so. If we ran up to them, scolding and waving our arms, all they did was laugh and wave back. But Dekking they respected as a dominant male. When he rushed at them, thumping a stick on the ground or rattling it among the trees, they were impressed indeed and climbed the nearest tree in a flash. Even the most obtuse orang got the message when Dekking said it was bed-time.

Once in the safety of the trees their mood might change; now they could smack their lips in threat, and even shake branches at us with energetic snorts. They reminded us of rebellious children, first resisting the order to go to bed, then going but slamming the door behind them.

The small orangs that were not yet ready for the trees retired to the rehabilitation cages for the night. Olip would sit on a heap of leaves and branches, his lower lip drawn in hard between his teeth, with the upper lip hanging slack over it. This was his 'evening face'; he adopted a particular grimace for a few succes-sive nights, then changed it for another. Several of the orangs made funny faces when they were playing on their own. The big, soft mobile lips and muscular faces lend themselves to it,

146

but we could never see why they did it. Face-making varied from one individual to another, and they seldom seemed to imitate each other. Purba's favourite evening face for a long time was to stick out his lips in the shape of a tube, like Donald Duck, and gaze expectantly at me. If I stroked his face, he would straightaway roll over in delight and chuckle happily.

There would be some last-minute games in the cages. Oyang had a special trick of taking a forked stick and fishing for bananas from the neighbouring cage. Orangs often use sticks as tools, even selecting them or breaking them so they are the right length for the job in hand. Wild orangs use such tools to reach distant fruits in trees, or to hook a branch from a neighbouring tree that they cannot reach otherwise. Oyang was very persistent, and often managed to hook a banana to see him through the night. But most by this time were ready for sleep. They would arrange the branches we provided in the semblance of a nest, and settle down happily for the night.

A thing that never failed to intrigue us was the orangs' knack for technology. They are renowned among zoo keepers for persistent fiddling with objects and materials, often with destructive results. This makes them harder to keep in cages than bigger and stronger apes. Gorillas hammer with their big fists on glass and walls, and hurl themselves bodily against the bars, using their great strength and weight. Orangs sit quietly in a corner and work away ceaselessly with their fingers, loosening screws, lifting planks – gradually taking the whole cage to pieces. Some of our orangs used branches and planks to bend bars apart, and devised levers to force padlocks and prize up floor boards. A complex lock or catch fascinates them, just as a camera or any new, complicated piece of apparatus had to be examined and twiddled before it can be left alone. Some of our orangs were especially intrigued when the carpenters came to repair their cages. They watched eagerly as the men worked near them and imitated when they could, using stones to hammer nails in and

147

'sawing' and 'planing' with sticks. Once Oyang, a particularly bright 4-year-old, acquired a saw and set about using it properly, expertly holding a board in the right position with one foot and one hand, and moving his body and sawing arm in a passable imitation of the workmen.

Because they are peaceable and introverted, orangs sometimes give the impression of being slow-witted and indolent. For a long time they were thought to be less intelligent than other apes. But research on orangs in zoos has shown them to be superior to gorillas and even equal to chimpanzees in solving problems. Some are capable of quite sustained thought. Jürgen Lethmate, who studied the tool-using behaviour of captive orangs, investigated their ability to join sticks together and 'fish' for things they wanted. He found, too, that they could work out how to pile boxes on top of each other to reach bananas hanging above their heads. To test their abilities for sustained thought he devised a set of three boxes with perspex windows and locked lids. In the first box he put a jar of fruit yoghurt – especially prized by the orangs he was testing. The key to this box was in the second box, and the key for the second box he placed on the cage floor. Alongside it was the key to the third box, which contained liquorice sweets – a reward, but nowhere near so popular as the yoghurt. It was relatively easy to get the liquorice, but a more complex and sustained process to get the yoghurt. The astonishing thing is that the orangs nearly always worked out how to get the yoghurt by thinking, not by trial. They were clearly able to compare the prizes and the difficulties of reaching them, and then follow through the sequence to get what they wanted.

Our orangs at Bohorok, like those in some of the better zoos, had plenty of materials around them to play with and activities to stimulate their minds. They may even have had more stimulation and opportunity for invention than they would have had in the wild. With regular feeding they had more leisure to play, and with more things to manipulate they had more opportunities for stretching their intelligence. It made me wonder why they had this spare capacity for thinking and using their brains, and how they would develop it if we – mankind – gave future generations of orangs the chance to continue their life in the rain forest.

14
Catching Orangs

The months passed quickly at Bohorok. Christmas came and went, and both Regina and I flew home to Switzerland for short spells of leave. Markus continued his studies of rhinoceroses, dropping in from time to time and then disappearing back into the forest. In February 1975 his work was completed, but he stayed on to complete a survey of tigers that he had already started, one which was to take him all over Sumatra. We had more visitors, gave more lectures, increased our local staff to three, and travelled further in search of orangs. More timber concessions were granted, more trees fell to the lumber-men's saws. The PPA redoubled its efforts to save orangs made homeless by the felling, and more displaced animals ended up – homeless and bewildered – in the quarantine cages at Bohorok.

Closer to home the durians ripened again, and we ran into trouble with our neighbours. One day in June there appeared on the station the *Kepala kampung* – village elder or headman – of the the nearby settlement of Gotong Royong. He was in truculent mood, his words backed by the community he represented.

'Your orangs are a nuisance,' he said. 'They are eating all our durians. They have got into our plantation and are picking the fruits before they fall to the ground. They have been there 3 weeks and already they've done a lot of damage.'

'How many of them are there?'

'Three, one big one and two small ones. They have eaten around 300 durian. We get 50 to a 100 rupiahs each for the fruit, so you'll have to pay us at least 150,000 rupiahs damages'.

That meant around £250 – a substantial slice of our budget. I was shocked, and I had to think quickly.

'How do you know that it's orangs from the station? Haven't you ever had problems before with wild apes?'

'Yes, of course we have. But in the old days we could always shoot them or catch them; now we can't do that any more. That's what you're here for. You're responsible for all these orangs, and you'll have to pay.'

I hadn't quite seen our work in that light before, and it took some getting used to. He had a point – several good points – and we'd have to do something about it quickly if we wanted to restore good neighbourly feeling. But there was a gleam in the headman's eye and I sensed – rightly or wrongly – that he and the villagers were trying it on. Never before had they been able to sell their durians for a guaranteed price before they were ripe, without even the trouble of picking them up and loading them onto the bus for market. I had a lot of sympathy for them, but this was a bit much.

'Why have you waited 3 weeks before coming to see us? Why haven't you tried to chase the animals away?'

'We didn't dare frighten your orangs.' This was a master-stroke: we both appreciated and relished its cunning. But I could be cunning too.

'It makes no difference whether they are wild or station orangs', I put it to him, 'They don't belong to us, they belong to you – to Indonesia. You are just as responsible for them as we are.'

I certainly felt for the peasants whose valued and favourite fruit the orangs were eating. And there was no doubt that the presence of the station increased the local population of orangs considerably. But I knew that paying up would not solve the problem. The orangs would just go on stuffing themselves to

the last durian, and next year they would be back for more; a
fairyland feast like this would be part of orang folk-lore – they'd
be bound to remember it. There was only one way out of this
mess. We would have to catch the animals and try and re-locate
them somewhere in the depths of the reserve.

'We'll see if we can get the PPA's permission to catch the
orangs and let them loose somewhere else. But we can't pay you
for the damage they've done. If they come into the plantations
you must chase them off. Or send for us straightaway; don't
wait until they've ravaged half your crop.'

The headman wasn't entirely satisfied with the turn the
argument had taken, but like all good negotiators, he knew
when to stop. All he could do was to accept our offer. As soon as
we had got the Conservancy Authority's permission, we set off
with a small team of local men – hastily recruited as ape-
catchers – to see what we could do for the villagers.

The three orangs had certainly made a mess of the durian
grove. Green fruit, bitten or torn in half, lay all over the ground.
In several trees they had built nests, for which of course they
had had to gather still more durian branches. It must have
seemed like paradise to them, to lie in their nests and gaze at
these prickly delicacies hanging all round them within reach.
We quickly came upon the first orang. He looked as well-fed
and prosperous as we expected, and he was not going to let our
arrival spoil his fun. We knew him. He was Momok, one we had
released at the station some months earlier. As he had been in
captivity only a few weeks before coming to us, we had let him
pass through Bohorok quickly. On release he had gone off on
his own immediately. He was a wily animal who knew all about
plantations before Bohorok; after some weeks with us he was
even less scared of living close to civilization where the pickings
were good.

While our catchers made ready and stretched out the nets, we
learnt from the villagers that orangs had come here every year to
steal durians, but there was something different about these

three: no matter how often you drove them away, they just waited patiently and swooped back as soon as they could. I was fairly certain they must all be Bohorok graduates, and I couldn't see any way out of the difficulty – short of getting the State to buy the plantation and incorporate it in the Reserve. This was Regina's idea, and the more we thought about it, the more it appealed to us. And if the orangs we released were not dispersing as we hoped they would, we'd have to take more active steps toward dispersing them – releasing them far away from Bohorok in the forested depths of the Reserve. But back to the job in hand.

We netted the three miscreants without much difficulty. The technique was to inveigle each one in turn into a single tree that could easily be isolated by lopping off neighbouring branches. The first we recognized as Mulya, a 6-year-old male whom Gersom had sent us from Aceh. I remembered him as a cheerful character who had left us only a few months before. Mulya let himself be driven with good humour, but soon lost his nerve, swinging around excitedly we cut off his retreat. Then one of the catchers climbed up the tree after him and began to harass him by shouting and shaking branches. Mulya wasn't used to this and seemed to consider it unfriendly. He grew even more excited and tumbled quickly down the tree, trying to make a dash for it across the ground. The nets were over him in no time. He stuck arms, head and legs through the wide mesh in an effort to escape, getting himself and the nets into a proper tangle. I gave him a tranquillizing shot in the shoulder that put him out in an instant. We carefully disentangled him and checked him for injuries, and Dekking and I carrried him to the village on a makeshift stretcher – a rice sack slung between two poles. Meanwhile Regina and the catchers went after the other two apes.

Our way to the village took us through an old rubber plantation and some small vegetable gardens to a point where we had to cross the Bohorok. There was a bridge, but it was no more than bamboo poles lashed together, extending over 70 feet of turbulent water with nothing to hang on to. I didn't trust myself to carry a sleeping orang across this slippery swaying affair, but it didn't worry Dekking. He picked up the 50 pounds or so of ape on one shoulder and tripped over, surefootedly as a ballet dancer. I followed gingerly, using the folded stretcher – to Dekking's amusement – like a tight-rope walker's pole.

In the village the crates stood ready. Carefully we laid the still sleeping Mulya on his side in one of them, with his face towards the window grille so that he could easily breathe fresh air. We closed and padlocked the lid. Dekking and one of the men carried the crate back to the station, while I returned to see how things were going in the durian grove. The second orang turned out to be a half-grown female – Betina – who had also been released from Bohorok after a short period of captivity. When I saw her she was hanging on to the extreme end of a branch 10 feet or so above ground, while one of the men, who had shinned up the trunk, was shouting and waving his arms at her. The man lopped the branch off with his parang, and Betina crashed down with it. Before she knew what was happening the nets were over her, and she too travelled to the village asleep on a stretcher. Momok was older and more wily, but we caught him the same afternoon. By the end of the day all three were sleeping off their tranquillizers in the comfort of the quarantine cages.

The villagers were reasonably happy with the outcome. We had accepted some responsibility and shown ourselves willing to help them, even if we couldn't offer full compensation. The orangs had gone, and the rest of the durians could ripen in peace. But the problem was still with us. Trudging wearily through the plantation in the late afternoon, carrying a blissfully unconscious ape on a stretcher, I had time to reflect that our orangs would continue to appear in plantations and gardens in the Bohorok area so long as we continued to accumulate them around the station. It was time – high time – for a helicopter release.

But there were more urgent matters to see to first. In July we were called out to the area between Besitang and Kuala Simpang, where the forests were being cut down at a great rate. Many timber concessions had been granted, and a lot were being worked simultaneously. As soon as the logs (destined mostly for plywood) were on their way to the factory in Besitang, local villagers moved in to burn off the undergrowth and raise crops on the open ground. Aerial surveys showed us a pattern of shrinking stands of trees, isolated by cultivation from the remaining blocks of virgin forest. In several of these stands lived orangs – lone males or small family groups of two or three. One large male in particular had been making a nuisance of himself by raiding the crops, and we were asked to remove him.

It was the village elder of Besitang who had sought our help, and we had agreed to try mainly in the hope of saving the orang and transferring him to the Reserve before the last of his forest home was cut from under him. After a 5-hour trip over bumpy roads, and endless asking-round in the village and its outlying settlements, we finally found somebody who knew where the ape was. Our guide led us along muddy forest tracks, full of puddles and mud from the passage of heavy equipment. Except for the track, the forest in places seemed almost untouched, but a small diversion to left or right always brought us to freshly-cut clearings or lumber camps: most of it had already been carved up and the rest would follow soon. It was a good hour before we finally reached the foot of the giant tree which was the orang's home.

It was an exceptionally tall tree. The spreading branches of its crown rose above all the other trees around it, hanging thick with brown pods whose seeds were probably its main attraction. Surrounded by food, the orang had woven himself a broad, deep nest almost in the middle of the crown; when he retired for his midday nap he was completely hidden from the ground. Though the buzz-saws were whining less than a quarter of a mile away, he would still have no idea that his home was threatened. He had probably lived there for twenty years or more, and knew no other kind of life. But fate had caught up: his section of forest was due to fall before the end of the week. We sat in the undergrowth, watching the felling operations. The lumberjacks wiped the sweat from their brows, yellow helmets gleaming in the sun. Shouts and warnings of falling trees were drowned by the whine of the saws and the sharp clatter of axes. One after another the giant trees fell, first in slow motion, then faster and faster, tearing others down with them and splintering their trunks. Bulldozers dragged the fallen trunks away and cleared new roads to other parts of the forest; small trees were ground to pulp in their tracks. There was an all-pervading smell of oil, exhaust fumes and freshly cut wood. Everywhere the reddish and yellowish stumps reared up among shattered branches and withering leaves.

The ape slept on in his nest high above. Perhaps he had spotted us, but hoped we would go away if he took no notice. Around Regina and me squatted a dozen or so men, some from Besitang, others who had come with us from Bohorok. The head of the party was an old, emaciated fisherman whose lively eyes twinkled in a deep-tanned face. In earlier days, around 1960, he had helped a Dutch zoologist and trapper to catch orangs and other primates. He still had his catching equipment – fine-meshed nets of thin wire rope, tied at the edges to a springy frame of bamboos.

Now the foresters moved across and began operations on the trees close to the nest. This was the signal for our own team to start work. First they cut down all the trees surrounding the giant, so that our prey would have no means of escape through the tree tops. Their shouts, the blows of the axes and the cracking of the trees as they fell still had no obvious effect on the orang; he stayed out of sight in his nest. Finally only the three largest trees remained surrounding the orang's tree, one of them hard up against it. When the men started on the furthest of these, the ape suddenly appeared, climbing uneasily with downward glances from the nest to the top of the crown.

Remorselessly the axes continued. '*Awas, jatuh*' ('Look out, its falling') shouted someone, and the first of the three supporters crashed to the ground. As the last branches were settling the great orang stretched to his full height in the crown of his own tree and pursed his lips in the form of a trumpet. From the depths of his throat rolled dark resounding calls like deep, resonant sighs. It was not the first time we had heard the 'long call' of the male orang, but we had never heard it so close, or uttered in such a situation of despair. It was as though the orang utan – the 'man of the forest' – had at last realized that his home was endangered, and the long, resonant call was his only defence.

He called again as the second tree fell, and again – a final despairing lament – as the third swished down, leaving only his own tree standing.

The men fell silent as the long calls rang out, and remained subdued while they cleared the undergrowth around the tree. Now the big orang was completely marooned. To leave his own tree and reach the rest of the forest, he would have to come down and cross at least 25 metres of open ground. That is where we hoped to catch him. But how would we get him down? Felling the tree would kill him. Starve him out? As though in answer to this point, the great ape collected a few handfuls of pods, from the dozens surrounding him, carried them to his nest, and settled down comfortably. He was far better prepared for a siege than we were, and seemed to know it. Dusk fell and we crept away, leaving three of the party on watch. There would be no more action that night.

At first light we speeded back along the muddy track, worried in case the orang had escaped in the night. But there he was, still sitting in his nest and munching a breakfast of husks. We settled down for a long wait in a circle of hides around the clearing. Extra branches draped above made us invisible to the orang – or so we hoped. Already strong, the sun burned down on the little bare patch of ground around the ape's tree. Apart from the chirping of crickets and cicadas, all was quiet. Our legs began to hurt from being doubled up, and the team of catchers, less patient than we were, became restless in the growing heat.

Eventually they devised a plan. It was to disturb the orang so violently and noisily that he would lose his nerve and come down from the tree. I had nothing better to offer, so I let them go ahead. With much shouting and shrieking they started to tug at a liana which, 20 metres long, ran close to the orang's nest and hung down almost to the ground. Three of them shook it violently rocking it to and fro and calling '*Turun, turun*' ('Come down'). The orang stood this for a time and then lost patience. With one strong hand he too grabbed the liana, shook it and pulled it toward him. The three terrified men at the other end, lifted bodily, let go and rolled to safety on the ground.

Next the men thought up a trick. Using thin trunks and branches, they made a framework 6 or 7 feet high and leaned it against the orang's tree, the way the native lumberjacks do. In these parts trees have to be cut several feet above the ground because of the enormous buttresses at the base of the trunk. One of the catchers climbed onto the frame and started to swing his axe against the tree with rhythmic blows, but using the blunt edge. The idea was to give the orang the impression that the tree was being felled, in the hope that he would take fright and try to escape. The rest of us returned to our hides to wait and see what would happen.

It soon became apparent that the trick was working. The great ape obviously didn't like what was going on. He looked around. We had hidden, so except for the man swinging the axe below, all was quiet. At last, as the blows continued steadily, he decided to come down. With wide-spread arms he climbed slowly down the lianas that hung from the thick trunk. Foot by foot he descended, hesitantly, slowly, stopping and looking around again and again. Regina and I held our breath: the men crouched in their hides, with nets poised ready to spring.

The 'lumberjack' continued to swing his axe, although he was obviously growing uneasy about the 200 pounds or so of unpredictable orang closing in on him from above. Now the animal stopped again. He spent several minutes looking carefully about the clearing. My heart was thumping so much that I thought he must have heard it. What a crazy thing to do – to try to catch an adult male orang practically with our bare hands! He'd certainly put up a fight – maybe he would attack us . . . or perhaps he'd climb his tree again and decide to sit it out.

Then he descended quickly down the last few metres. Level with the 'lumberjack' he paused a moment; man and ape exchanged frightened glances, and he hastily continued his descent. Reaching the foot of the tree he dropped to the ground and ran quickly on all fours towards the furthest corner of the clearing. This was precisely the one direction where no one sat ready for him; clearly, his careful scrutiny on the way down had told him the exact position of all our hides.

In a flash men with nets and sticks were running at him from all sides. We ran too, tranquillizer syringes at the ready. The men caught up with him and managed to throw two nets over him. He spread out his mighty arms and the nets slid from this shoulders. Then, as he reached with his hand for the safety of a little tree, someone threw the net again. Again he brushed it aside and drew back, confused by the horde of shouting enemies who faced him two metres away. Now the fear showed clearly on his great flat face. As one of the men poked excitedly at him with a stick, he leaped up into the little tree – it almost collapsed under him – and thence onto a bigger one close by. Then he was away, far above our heads and out of our reach. On the ground below everyone sat down and began an excited discussion, arguing how they could have done it better; the tension was quickly broken and the men lit up and laughed. Regina and I sat quietly, still excited, sadly disappointed, but deeply impressed by the performance of this splendid animal that had got away from us. Never had an orang made me more acutely conscious of the gentleness and lack of agression that rule the lives of these great red apes. Despite its enormous strength and undoubted ability to bite and tear with its teeth, this orang made no attempt to attack his tormentors – or even to feign an attack. How easy it would have been for him to do what any gorilla or chimpanzee – or even man – would have done, faced with such a desperate and dangerous situation. But, obviously nothing but flight was in his mind; he even had to turn his back to us to climb the tree that led to his escape.

I still wonder why orang utans do not defend themselves more effectively in moments of real danger. Physically they certainly have the means to do so, but their peace-loving nature just doesn't seem able to adjust to it. Zoo orangs often become dangerous to their keepers because they have learned from experience that they are the stronger. But measuring strength in this way seems to be far from the minds of wild orangs. Their reactions to the unknown are curiosity or anxiety, never agression. Could it perhaps be that as tree dwellers they have no enemy – other than us humans?

Our gentle giant did not flee far. The excitement of the morning seemed to have worn him out, and he soon built himself a nest. This time four men kept watch through the night under his tree while the rest of us went back to the village. Despite the inadequacy of our equipment we wanted to have another try to catch this big orang the next day. We planned to make a larger clearing so that he would have further to run, and have more men standing by to hold the nets and pin them firmly to the ground. We spent much of the night making plans, and rushed back expectantly the next day all ready to start again.

But we learned on arrival that the orang had been making plans too. In the grey light of dawn he had swung off into the forest: though the watchers tried to follow him, they soon lost him as he moved easily along his tree-top tracks. We searched the whole day, then decided to go back to Bohorok and return for a further round with larger and more suitable nets.

Sadly, we never saw that particular orang again. He seemed to have got away through fields and stands of timber, perhaps to regain the main body of the forest. But despite his experience and obvious ability to look after himself, successful escape probably meant disaster rather than salvation, for more and more of the forest in that region is coming down in the next few years. He probably shares the fate of at least thirty or forty other orangs and numerous families of gibbons and siamangs that live around Besitang; deprived of anywhere to settle, they will be delivered over to hunger and persecution, and must all die long before their time.

15
Dispersal

Taking stock of the programme we had worked out for returning orangs to the jungle, we could see in retrospect that we had
planned it as a three-stage operation. If, in the early days, we
had written a rehabilitation manual for ourselves and the orangs
to follow, it would have contained three sections – we might
have called them quarantine, resettlement and release. Quarantine, simply enough, was the period of 6 to 12 weeks when the
newly-acquired animals, housed singly or in pairs in roomy
cages, were sized up, cleaned up, treated medically for worms
and other parasites and diseases, and fed to capacity. The result
was usually a healthy ape, relieved of most of the illnesses and
problems arising out of its former captivity. A few were ready
for immediate release into the forest, but many – especially the
youngest – still had some way to go.

The second stage – resettlement – took place in the rehabilitation cages up on the ridge. Here our animals were still in cages,
but far more isolated from human influences. We kept an
eye on them several times a day, but mainly from a distance.
For most of each day they were surrounded entirely by the
sounds and smells of the forest, and could see their more
advanced colleagues moving about in complete freedom
among the trees. How long this stage lasted depended entirely on individual response. For some it was no more than a
fretful 2 or 3 days, for others several weeks under lock and key

until we were satisfied that they were competent to live independently.

The third stage – freedom – was interpreted in different ways by the orangs themselves. Some took full advantage of it from the first moment, disappearing through the trees like scalded cats without a single backward glance. These were mostly strong-minded animals whose captivity had been short and untraumatic. We welcomed their show of independence. It boded well; we were sure they would find a place for themselves in the forest, and hoped it would be far from Bohorok.

Others less certain of themselves took to a system of day-release, leaving the cages when we unlocked them in the mornings, but staying close by and returning at night. We made them welcome with food and bedding; they were clearly not yet ready for complete freedom, and it would not have made sense for us to force them away, or leave them loose in the forest at night, if they did not feel competent to deal with the situation themselves. Day-release did not usually last long. Most of our animals relished their freedom and took very quickly to the world outside the cages. They remained free, but hung about for several weeks, often disappearing for a few days and then returning one tea-time in the hope of a free meal. We were always glad to see them – their return in good health meant that they were coping well on their own – but we kept them at a distance and gave them as few opportunities as possible to become habituated at the food table.

That some of our orangs returned from time to time did not dismay us; they were learning their independence gradually, and that was a good thing. The ones that concerned us most were the orangs who stayed for months around Bohorok, taking up permanent residence close to the station and descending on us all too frequently for company and a chance of food. These, we felt, were playing the system to its limits. Apart from their incursions into the local plantations, they were probably competing with each other and with newly-released animals, to the detriment of all. Our job with them was not yet finished. We had to take them from Bohorok and disperse them in the Reserve.

So we added a fourth stage – dispersal – to our programme of rehabilitation. It was a problem that had struck us quite early on in our studies; indeed our excursion to the headwaters of the Bohorok (chapter 7) had been partly to see how possible it might be to release orangs in that direction. The main difficulty was transportation. Ideally we needed to move them at least 20 km from the station toward the centre of the Langkat Reserve, preferably putting a river or a mountain range between us as a barrier to their return. But the reserve had no roads – only a few tracks, and mostly very doubtful ones, as we had discovered; crossing it on foot with a cargo of crated orangs was almost impossible. The only effective routes into the reserve were the rivers, all of them treacherous in the extreme. I was not willing to trust orangs to the rivers. Once we had almost lost one in crossing the river by the station; the orang in its crate had rocked the boat and toppled into the water. Everyone jumped in after it and the orang was saved. But I didn't like to think of a similar happening during a release expedition.

Helicopter flights were the obvious alternative, but here the trouble was cost. We could occasionally rent a helicopter for a few hours from one of the local oil companies, but they were busy people with other things on their minds. We had managed one trip with them in September 1974, disposing successfully of Doli, Mania and three other of our early acquisitions. Now, toward the end of my stay at Bohorok, we felt it was time for another journey by air to the centre of the reserve, with a second load of orangs for dispersal.

Opportunity came with the arrival of the Anglia Television team in June 1975. Happy with the chance of filming the whole performance, they generously offered to rent a helicopter and help with all the arrangements for the release. Dieter Plage and Mike Price, the two wildlife cameramen of 'Survival's' unique team, were thorough professionals with a wide experience of filming animals in the wild. Intrigued by the orangs, and very much in sympathy with our work, they spent hours filming at the cages and in the open forest, and were constantly on the look-out for sequences of activity that would help the story-line of their 'Survival' film. They came with us when we collected orangs from captivity, were present when we netted Momok and his accomplices in the gardens at Gotong Royong, and crouched long hours on specially-built tree hides – often in heavy rain – photographing the animals climbing, swinging, feeding, quarrelling, and sheltering from the weather. Filming the final release was an interesting end-point for their work, and provided an excellent sequence for the movie.

We selected eight of our band for dispersal. All were between four and ten years old. Five of them had been living for some months in complete freedom without being fed by us. Though fully rehabilitated, they had made their home too near us for comfort, and we felt they would be better in the complete isolation of the central reserve. Two days before the flight was due we tempted the free ones into a cage and locked them up, so that we wouldn't have to be hunting them while the helicopter stood waiting. Also on our list were Momok, Mulya and Betina, the three delinquents of Gotong Royong. They had been caged since we caught them in the durian plantation some weeks before: we hadn't dared to release them, as they would certainly have made their way back to continue their feast.

Momok, ten years old with a beautiful moon-face and light beard, crouched in a corner of his cage when we came to transfer him to his travelling crate. Though wild enough in a durian garden, he was shy and retiring in captivity; his weight and strength made it necessary for me to tranquillize him for the transfer. He hid his face as I approached, and I was already injecting the drug into his thigh muscles before he realized what was happening. In a moment he was sleepy, and in minutes he relaxed into a deep sleep, allowing us to lift him gently into the travelling crate. Mulya and Betina, six or seven years old, shared a cage and tended to jump and display when we approached, swinging nervously about from wall to wall with a noisy smacking of lips. We caught them by stealth. One of the helpers entered the back of the cage, driving the orangs to the front bars. From cover we leapt out and grabbed them through the bars, giving small doses of tranquillizer that sedated without making them fully unconscious. Then we transferred them without difficulty to the travelling crates, where they recovered within the hour.

Pandi and Pesek, the next two candidates, had been inveigled in from the tea-party. Pesek, who was once everybody's friend, by this time allowed only Dekking to come close and touch him. Dekking placed some particularly luscious fruit in a travelling crate and led Pesek toward it. Pesek climbed in obligingly, and was feeding happily when the lid came down. Pandi returned to the cage, and had to be mildly sedated before she would let herself be crated. So, on the evening before the flight, five of our orangs occupied a row of sturdy crates in a clearing by the station. That left Cabe, Pakam and Gamat, three gentle, quiet animals whom we knew could be handled easily both before and during the flight. To save space on the helicopter we wanted to avoid crating them; they would travel in sacks at the feet of the passenger in front. On the last night they too were caged, Pakam, the pretty 7-year-old, pouting through the bars as though about to burst into tears. Cabe, once a neurotic problem child who could not bear to be left, now played happily on the floor of the cage with Gamat, who accepted her temporary captivity philosophically.

The bearers appeared at first light – a group of tough young men from Bukit Lawang. Pairing off, they tied the five crates with nylon ropes to stout bamboo staves, which they lifted onto their shoulders. Slowly, and with much uneasy swaying, the orangs were carried across the river and through the wood to the village, where we had arranged for the helicopter to land on the large football field nearby. Gamat and Pakam walked down the forest track, led by the hand; they made no fuss about getting into the boat, sitting quietly on the seats while Dekking steered them across the river, then continuing down to the village on foot. I followed with Cabe on my arm. This was the last time ever that I would carry him, and I was happy to see that being carried gave him little pleasure; no longer dependent on human contact, he would just as soon have jumped away from me and taken a premature trip into the trees on his own behalf. On the landing ground all three climbed into their sacks without fuss, and waited patiently, like airline passengers the world over, for their flight to be called.

The Alouette 3 helicopter was standing ready on the football field, with an excited crowd milling around it. Two trips were needed to carry the crates, the sacks, the camera team and all their gear; I travelled on the second flight, with the three orangs draped in their sacks about my legs. They remained very quiet for the 10 minutes or so in the air. Only Gamat, puzzled and a little angry, took a snap now and again at anything in reach; once it was Cabe, and once my leg, but the thick sacking softened her bite. The flight along the river was dreamlike in its beauty. Like a great dragonfly the helicopter hummed its way up the valley, sometimes so close above the tree tops that I involuntarily drew my feet up. It was like swinging over the forest in a soap bubble, with only the roar of the engine shattering the illusion.

We landed in the middle of the reserve at a point known locally as Simpang Dua – the place where two rivers join. The helicopter touched down gently on a dry shingle bank, where a party of bearers was already waiting for us; they had come up on foot the day before, and had prepared a camp where we could stay for two or three days to see the orangs safely into the forest. Our second load, including the three sacks – now moving restlessly like three disorderly caterpillars – was quickly unshipped, and we all hugged the ground while the helicopter

167

rose, circled, and sped back to civilization. As the drone of its engine faded we heard the natural forest sounds of rushing water and whispering trees, and suddenly appreciated our position – in the middle of an undisturbed jungle reserve, one of the last in tropical south-east Asia, with only the river to lead us home.

Our first job was to release the orangs. We carried the crates and sacks across the river and deep into virgin forest, a quarter of an hour's walk from the river bank. Lianas as thick as my arm hung from the tall, heavily branching trees, many of which were thickly encrusted with fruit; to us at least it seemed an orangs' paradise. Sunlight filtered dimly through the tree tops, leaving the group in semi-darkness. It was difficult to remember the vivid early morning light we had left behind only a few minutes ago. We walked a narrow path, made by the advance party on the previous day, through dense undergrowth on a carpet of soft, rotting humus, to a point in the forest where Dieter and the men had built a camera platform and hide well above ground level. This was a vantage point, thought out with thoroughness beforehand, from which Dieter could photograph the orangs as they climbed to freedom.

As Dieter scrambled up to his eyrie and prepared the camera for action, we waited impatiently on the ground. Even the orangs were beginning to lose their customary patience; the sacks were rolling and turning somersaults, and had to be tied down until Dieter was ready. Then I opened the first sack, closely followed by the second and third, and stood back to watch.

Gamat was first out; she slipped straightaway from her sack and fled into the trees. Only at a safe height of 7 or 8 metres did she stop to look around, then climbed on as though the furies themselves were behind her. Cabe and Pakam too shinned up the lianas, though with less urgency. Perhaps they had found the journey less distressing, for they soon got over it; within minutes they were relaxing in the branches immediately over our heads, eating leaves and watching our activities with interest. Next we let Pandi out of her crate. We had often seen her around the station in the company of Pakam or Gamat, and we hoped the three would be company for each other at least during the first few days of their exile. Pandi climbed high and moved away, shortly to be joined by both Pakam and Gamat, and the three disappeared together into the forest.

Next it was the turn of the two friends Betina and Mulya. Both of them shot up the lianas, snatching only a hasty glance back. They too recovered quickly from the journey; in a few minutes they were hanging head-downward and sparring playfully together, just as we had often seen them at Bohorok. Then they climbed slowly on; I caught a last glimpse of them 50 or 60 metres away before they finally disappeared from our view. Pesek was more circumspect. He emerged from the top of his crate and stopped to take a deliberate, careful look around. Then he reached for the nearest liana and began to climb it almost hesitantly, stopping frequently to look about him as though he could not quite believe his eyes. He too disappeared quickly into the trees, and we never saw him again.

That left Momok, the shy 10-year-old. Last to be released, Momok remained at the bottom of his crate as if he had washed his hands of the whole disturbing business. I stood back behind a tree and waited, well away from him and out of his line of sight. At last he changed his mind, suddenly emerging, ducking, and making a quick dash across the ground to disappear into the undergrowth. After a time I noticed some philodendron leaves moving a short distance away; this was Momok, climbing silently and shyly as ever up the far side of one of the trees, with only his long brown arms giving away his position.

In an hour or less all the orangs were freed to go their own way in the forest, and within another hour all but one had disappeared. The exception was Cabe. He discovered Dieter's hide and decided to explore its possibilities before leaving; he performed gymnastics all around it, and watched Dieter closely as he finished shooting his film. We left Cabe on his own, walking in single file back along the narrow tract to the river.

Our camp lay across the river – by design, so that we would have a natural barrier between us and the newly liberated orangs. The 'tent' was a framework of bamboos and saplings, covered against the weather by sheets of plastic but wide open at the front. There was a fireplace, built with stones from the river and protected by a lean-to roof, and a smoky fire that warmed a battered black tin pot full of rice. River fish that looked like trout were grilling on split bamboo stakes, and the tent contained a colourful mish-mash of clothes, camera boxes, food, crockery and men. Someone carved a wooden ladle and the fish and rice were served up on tin plates; it had been a long morning, and the food was welcome. We ate with our fingers – right hand only, in the world-wide tradition, forcing the fish and rice together into tasty balls which we ate with relish.

After lunch the men scattered with rods and *jalas* to catch fish for the evening meal, while Dieter, Mike and I returned along the forest path to the point where we had released the orangs. Apart from the shrilling of crickets there was nothing to be heard – no rustling of leaves or waving, crackling branches – to indicate the presence of orangs. We made a long sweep up the slopes above the river and stumbled along a ridge, to find a viewpoint from which we could see the tree-tops and the contours of the forest for miles in either direction. Then we returned to the river bank. We found no remains of food, no nests, in fact nothing at all to indicate the presence of eight lively orangs; it was as though they had vanished in the few hours since the release, and I began to feel that the whole release operation had been a long, elaborate dream.

It was Cabe who brought me back to reality. We found him again in Dieter's hide, where he was playing with nylon rope that Dieter had used to haul up his camera. He kept his distance, and gazed after us as we headed for home down the narrow forest track.

A quarter of an hour later we were back in the camp, with our wet shoes and socks dripping in front of the fire. The spicey scent of the moist rain forest mixed with the smoke of the fire and the homely smell of grilling fish; as dusk fell I felt curiously at home in our ramshackle camp. While supper cooked I walked up the river with soap and towel to find a secluded spot for bathing. I had to be particularly modest, for our bearers were Muslim and, to them, a glimpse of my nakedness – even by chance – would mean certain punishment in the life to come. They were far too nice to deserve such a fate, so I took good care to keep out of their sight while bathing.

I was just able to get back from my bath as the rain began to fall. For the men to share a tent with a woman provided a slight problem, but the proprieties were satisfied when they surrounded me with a little wall, less than a half a metre high, made up of camera cases. Then they could relax. Dieter and Mike generously offered me some of their tinned rations – sauerkraut, bean soup with sausages and pease pudding – but I opted for the wonderfully aromatic fish, rice and chilli-based vegetables that the men had prepared. The rain drummed steadily on the plastic roof, forming a glittering curtain between us and the forest and the night sky. The lanterns were lit, but it was too dark to read and I was too tired anyway. I curled up in my sleeping bag among the camera cases, listening to the quiet talking of the men as they smoked, gossiped and played cards. One by one they too retired, wrapping themselves in their sarongs and sleeping where they lay. I slept long and soundly.

We stayed a further 2 days in the forest, combing the area upstream and down in search of the orangs we had released. There was neither sight nor sound of any of them, except Cabe – who was still climbing about in the tree close to Dieter's hide, perhaps in the hope that we would return and keep him company. It was raining hard when we paid our final visit to the hide on the last evening of our stay. There was Cabe, still keeping his distance, on a branch just above the hide. He was holding an umbrella of leaves over his head with both hands, while the raindrops glistened on his wiry, rust-red hair.

We returned to Bohorok along the river, taking a full day to travel the distance that the helicopter had managed in 10 minutes. It was a laborious journey, crossing and re-crossing the stream on slippery pebbles with all our heavy gear. We finally reached the station 2 hours after nightfall. I have vivid memories of the last few miles of the journey, as the sun disappeared, colours dissolved into shades of grey, and darkness finally fell over the forest. It was a rough track, and we had only the dim light of a couple of torches to see us on our way. The air was cool and our wet clothes stuck clammily to us as we staggered through the darkness, dog-tired from our long day's march. I have never known our little station so welcoming, or our coffee taste so good, as on our return to Bohorok that night.

Epilogue

For Markus, Regina and me, Bohorok was almost over. Markus and I left late in 1975, returning to Europe for a year of travel and writing up. Regina stayed on for a few months, then handed the station over to two successors for most of 1976. I returned in December 1976 for a period of 4 months, and was able to hand over to another couple – Conrad and Rosalind Aveling – who took charge in March 1977.

Sitting at the feeding place on my last afternoon at Bohorok, I checked in my mind through the happenings of the past 4 years, pondering over what we had really achieved. Bohorok was a going concern; of that there was no doubt. The work was continuing, the buildings were serving their purpose, and orangs were still being brought in for rehabilitation. Since starting it up, over 50 orangs in varying states of mental and physical distress had been taken in, treated and released successfully. About half had been released by helicopter in the middle of the Langkat Reserve; the rest had left the station and disappeared in directions known only to themselves.

We could not be certain that the liberated orangs had survived; how could we tell, when they had disappeared into a trackless rain forest where there was no chance of following them? But we could guarantee that they were healthy animals when they left us, with all the skills they needed for survival. We had every reason to believe that they would be successful, and fully able to cope with their new life in the forest.

Fifty rehabilitated orangs – it didn't seem much compared with the total population of animals at risk in Sumatra. Of course the Rijksens and their successors were rehabilitating too, at about the same rate. Perhaps between us we had saved a hundred or more animals in the past 4 to 5 years. Estimates based on John MacKinnon's work and our own observations indicate that there are 4–5,000 orangs in the forests of Sumatra, all of them in the two northern provinces of Aceh and North Sumatra. About half of them live in the three great central reserves – the Gunung Leuser, Langkat and Kluet Reserves. The remaining 2,000 or more live outside the conservation areas, and their living space is being reduced daily by timber exploitation, forest clearance for plantations, and shifting cultivation. Apart from the ones that had passed through our hands, what had we done for these hundreds of orangs whose homes and livelihoods were constantly at risk?

Thinking about it in the heat of the sultry afternoon, and remembering back to our early days, I felt that we might well have helped them indirectly through our efforts at Bohorok. The Sumatran agency directly responsible for the welfare of orangs was the PPA. By linking our work with the PPA we had strengthened its hand – morally, perhaps, through the support of the World Wildlife Fund, and practically by providing a centre to which it could send confiscated orangs. Until Ketambe and Bohorok were established, there was little the PPA could do to enforce the law about keeping orangs in captivity or trading them. Our stations provided care and rehabilitation for confiscated animals – a reasonable alternative to the private collector, the poacher and the trader. The results were indisputable. Trading in orangs had virtually come to an end in northern Sumatra and on the west coast of Aceh; only in eastern Aceh, where the timber companies were most active and the PPA had no inspection posts, was poaching still a proposition. By now most of the inhabitants of both provinces had heard of our stations, and knew that the law concerning orangs was being taken seriously. We could be reasonably sure that, where the PPA was represented, disposessed animals would be brought to its notice and stand a fair chance of resettlement through Ketambe or Bohorok.

Perhaps, too, our presence had helped to convince the Indonesian Government that the world outside Indonesia regarded it as custodian of the orangs, and was interested in their welfare. So the Government might be persuaded to use the legislation at its disposal, to strengthen the agency (the PPA) directly responsible, and even to ensure that its timber resources were exploited in ways which were not entirely destructive to the orang populations. Bohorok, with its World Wildlife Fund signboard and Toyota, was a constant reminder of overseas interest in conservation, and we were but one of many specialist teams and agencies that were helping and advising in the protection of Indonesian flora and fauna.

I was encouraged to think that the idea of conservation has come to stay in Indonesia. The current 5-year plan, for example, provides for doubling the total area of reserves and – with international support – for improvement in the condition and standards of monitoring and protection in existing parks.

Deep in thought, I made my way for the last time from the feeding place down to the houses. In the gathering dusk it seemed as though the night was rising from the forest. I noticed things that I must have seen every day without recording – tiny plants that had rooted along the path, tender green leaves growing from the sprouting live timber of one of the steps. Tight roles of young fern fronds sprang from the dark foliage all around, and an unseen animal scampered off through the undergrowth. Suddenly I had the feeling of being watched. Four metres above me Purba, one of our oldest friends remaining at Bohorok, poked his head over the edge of his nest and smiled comfortably at me.

It had all been well worthwhile.

Acknowledgments

The Frankfurt Zoological Society finances most of the orang utan project at Bohorok. Without their help we could never have realized the project and I am especially indebted to Prof Dr Dr B. Grzimek and Dr R. Faust who backed it in good and bad times.

I am very happy and grateful that Survival Anglia have helped so much with this book. I enjoyed watching the shooting of the TV film 'Orang Utan' and I appreciated the company and good cooperation of the two cameramen Dieter Plage and Mike Price.

I wish to thank Dr Bernard Stonehouse for his invaluable assistance in accomplishing the book.

I am grateful to World Wildlife Fund International who helped with the sponsoring of the project and to L.I.P.I., the Scientific Research Council of Indonesia, who arranged for us to obtain the necessary permissions for our research.

Dinas P.P.A., the Indonesian Nature Conservation Department, have assisted our project in many ways. Among many other helpful P.P.A. –employees, I would like to thank especially Mr J. Bangun Mulya and Mr S. Poniran as well as Mr Dekking Bangun Mulya and Mr Daulat Purba, employees of the station who have worked with the project since the beginning.

Several medical doctors have helped to treat or operate on

sick orangs as well as on ourselves. Among them, I should like to mention especially Dr E Diehl, Dr E. N. Kosasih, Dr Nurwani Mako Salim, Dr Erwin Kadar, Dr Elisabeth Baumann and Dr Alex Landolt.

I am very grateful for the help we received from our many friends. Mrs Veronika von Stockar has assisted the project greatly by raising additional funds as well as by giving practical help at the station. Mr and Mrs Janssen have cared for sick or infant orangs, Mr and Mrs Albert Sulistyo have offered advice and shelter to us and our orangs on many occasions, and Mr and Mrs Rüesch have always been ready to offer help and a hospitable home. A large number of friends in Indonesia, Europe and the United States have helped us in many ways, and I am grateful to them all.

I am very grateful to my family, to our parents for their interest and understanding, and of course to Markus, my husband, whose advice and practical help were of great value.

Finally, I would like to thank Regina Frey for our good relationship and cooperation. I have been very happy working with her at Bohorok; our team-work which started as an experiment turned out to be a success.

Monica Borner
January 1979

Bibliography

Brindamour-Galdikas, Biruté: Orangutans, Indonesia's "People of the Forest". "National Geographic" 148 (4) 444–73. 1975.

Harrisson, Barbara: *Orang-Utan*. Collins, London 1962.

Horr, David Agee: *The Borneo Orang-Utan.* "Borneo Research Bulletin" 4 46–50. 1972
Orang-Utan Watching: A Day in the Life. "Borneo Research Bulletin", 5 7–10. 1973.

Lethmate, Jürgen: *Problemlöseverhalten von Orang-Utans (Pongo pygmaeus).* "Fortschritt Verhaltensforschung", (19) 1–70. 1977.

Rijksens, H.D.: Experiments carried out mainly at the Munster and Osnabruck zoos. A Fieldstudy on Sumatran Orang Utans (*Pongo pygmaeus abelii* Lesson 1827). "Ecology, behaviour and conservation". "Mededelingen Landbonnhogeschool" Wageningen 78–82, 1–420. 1978.

Rodman, P.S.: "Population composition and adaptive organisation among Orang-Utans of the Kutai Reserve". *Comparative Ecology and Behaviour of Primates.* 171–209. Editors, R. P. Michael & J. H. Crook, Academic Press, London 1973.

Index

(compiled by Arthur Windsor)

Borner, Berni, 120–1
Borner, Markus, cooking, 65–6;
and elephant, 26–7; and forest,
14–15; kidnaps Riau, 120–1;
Lake Bangko journey, 27–37;
marriage to author, 47–9,
59–61; and orang project, 5–7;
and Regina, 58–9; rhino project, 6, 27, 38, 58; expedition,
72–80, 120; ends, 150; and
Riau, 120–1; tiger survey, 150;
and Wumi, 58–9
Borner, Monica, author, begins
orang project, 3–6; goes to
Sumatra, 8; marriage to Markus, 47–9, 59–61; rhino expedition, 72–80; site for research
station found, 42; and *passim*
Boyle, Frederick, quoted, 35
Brindamour-Galdikas, Birouté,
5; and orang utan, 16
Brindamour-Galdikas, Ron, 5
Bukit Lawang, 42, 49, 54, 84
Bumi, orang, 94–5

Cabe, orang, 56, 57; dispersal,
166–72; finishes quarantine,
66–8; treatment at Bohorok,
68–70, 85
catching a wild orang, failure,
155–61
Chang, Chinese police informer,
128–9
Chindri, Mr — , and Untung,
116–17
climbing, orangs learn, 111–12
cockroaches, 132–3
Comel, orang, gets medical
treatment, 135–8

'day-release' and orangs, 163
Diehl, Dr, 139

Dinas Perlindungan dan Pengawetan Aam (PPA) *see* PPA
Doli, orang, 55; dispersal, 164;
finishes quarantine, 66–8;
steals a camera, 134–5; and
Wumi, 56–7, 70–1
Dolok Merangir, Goodyear plantation hospital in, 139
durian fruit, 51, 66; orangs steal,
150–3

elephant, in Sumatra, 26–7
Elisabeth — , Swiss doctor,
123–6; and Comel, 135–8
Erwin, Dr, saves Gareng's life,
103

Faust, Dr R., v
Frankfurt zoo, 6
Frankfurt Zoological Society
(Zoologische Gesellschaft von
1858), x, xi, 4, 6
Frey, Regina, 5, 7, 26; arrives in
Medan, 49–50; lecture tour,
Aceh, 123–6; and Markus,
58–9; rehabilitation and, 100,
104–5; wedding, 60–1; and *pas-
sim*

Gamat, orang, 71; behaviour,
141, 142; dispersal, 166–9
Gareng, orang rehabilitation,
101–4
Goodall, Jane, 106
Gotong Royong, miscreants of,
150–4, 165
Goyang, orang, 126–7
Grzimek, Bernhard, x
Grzimek, Michael, x
Gunung Leuser Reserve, vi, 10,
11, 14, 28, 39, 73, 174

Index